LIVING SENT

Justin Thomas Wester

Fitting Words

Praise for Living SENT

Justin Wester has written my favorite kind of book. It is visionary, honest and practical. In *Living SENT* he shares wise insights, asks good questions and invites the reader to take tangible action, in solidarity with others, to live as Jesus did. Anyone who dares to go on the journey this book describes will experience the joy of being dangerously alive.

Mark Scandrette, founding director of ReIMAGINE and author of
Practicing the Way of Jesus and The Ninefold Path of Jesus:
Hidden Wisdom of the Beatitudes.

Justin Wester is the real deal as he is both a thought leader & practitioner. *Living SENT* provides tools and resources for believers to engage the people we see every day. God is at work in the places we often overlook; our own households, neighborhoods, workplaces, and communities. This book will equip and inspire you to rediscover those places and love those whom God has put right in front of us.

Dave Runyon, co-author of *The Art of Neighboring*

In his book *Living SENT*, Justin Wester addresses much of what is hindering the Church from becoming a missional force. Unfortunately, somewhere along the way, the Western Church has become addicted to the "show" on Sunday mornings rather than living out the Great Commission throughout the week! *Living SENT* simply means that every believer is called to be an intentional evangelist and a multiplying disciple-maker in all their spheres of influence! Given that reality, through his book, Justin will help the church, your church, become gospel-driven again!

Dr. David A. Wheeler, Professor of Evangelism,
Sr. Executive Director of LU Shepherd, Rawlings School of Divinity

Justin Wester lays out the foundation for why *Living SENT* is so critical for the Church today. In a society where Christ followers are increasingly told our faith needs to be a private thing, *Living SENT* is a biblical, practical, and crucial exercise if believers are going to impact the world around them, and see friends, neighbors, co-workers – even people we simply connect with randomly – experience faith in Jesus Christ.

Sean McMahon, Executive Director, Florida Baptist Association

I can't think of a better way to equip people to follow Christ than the idea of what it means to live SENT. Justin Wester isn't just giving us his ideas or theories, but what he has actually implemented and practiced, leading his local church on mission with Jesus. I believe this book will be very helpful for local churches in their discipleship efforts. Please don't just read this book, but also use it to equip the church in following Christ.

Dean Inserra, Pastor, City Church, Tallahassee,
author of *The Unsaved Christian and Getting Over Yourself*

Dr. Wester has brought to the church a post-modern, post-Christian approach to evangelism that is scripturally deep and practically functional. Biblical evangelism is about life transformation (salvation) and the significance of living the transformed life (discipleship) with non-believers and church attendees (evangelism). *Living SENT* is a must read for effective evangelism in the 21st century.

Gary Townsend, North Florida Regional Catalyst,
Florida Baptist Convention

CONTENTS

FOREWORD

In his book *Leadership Without Easy Answers*, author Ronald Heifetz distinguishes between organizational change and cultural change. He argues that organizational change typically involves a restructuring of some type, along with new programs, processes, and techniques. Cultural change, however, looks at how to create a new culture or environment, which will, in turn, require an entirely new set of skills and capacities.

This topic of cultural change is important for the church because the answer to the crisis of the church in North America will not be found by making organizational changes. We can't settle with minor adjustments in our ecclesiology or how we *do* church. Instead, the problem is much more deeply rooted. We must look to make cultural changes. The underlying issues are primarily spiritual, theological, and missiological. To lead disciple-making, missional-incarnational churches with the mindset of community transformation will take deep cultural change in the way we think about God's mission and the nature of the church, and how the church engages in that mission in local contexts.

Another way to frame the discussion is to use the language of *paradigm*. The word paradigm commonly refers to a perception, assumption, or frame of reference. In the more general sense, it's simply how we see the world in terms of perceiving, understanding, and interpreting.

Every organization, including the church, is built upon underlying paradigms or assumptions. This is not the same thing as the church's beliefs or theological systems. Rather the paradigm determines how an organization thinks and, therefore, acts. Paradigms explain and then guide behavior. If we try to restructure an organization but leave the original paradigms in place, nothing will change *within* the organization. Therefore, for real change to take place, we need to experience a paradigm shift or, in most cases, multiple paradigm shifts.

A paradigm shift happens when there is a fundamental change in an underlying assumption. It's a change from one way of thinking to another. There is a transformation or a sort of metamorphosis that takes place. Now, in the context of our understanding of church and mission, there are at least two reasons we need to experience this type of genuine paradigm shift.

First, those who have been "churched" for a long time typically have some deeply held assumptions about church and mission that may no longer be appropriate in a post-Christendom context. Often these assumptions need to be challenged, or at least investigated, to ensure they are still correct.

Second, cultural change, and ultimately organizational change, will not last if it isn't rooted in paradigm-shift thinking. Without re-establishing certain theological foundations that help us "unlearn and relearn," we naturally default toward making modest tweaks in how we operate, rather than cutting to the deeper issues of why.

One final thought on the importance of paradigm thinking. An adage that speaks to the importance of considering change in an organization goes like this: We are perfectly designed to achieve what we are currently achieving. If we apply this statement to the church today, one question we might ask would be: Are we satisfied with what we are currently achieving? In other words, are we content or pleased with the impact the church is having today? If we are totally honest, the answer would seem to be a resounding *"No!"*

The fact is, regardless of what marker a person looks at to judge the health of the church in North America, every indicator is trending in the wrong direction. If we are perfectly designed to achieve what the church is currently achieving, shouldn't we ask if there is an issue in the way we are designed? Or at least question if there is an issue in the way we understand the nature of the church and its place in God's mission? Are there design factors that we need to rethink to achieve the outcomes we desire?

The strategies and techniques that fit previous eras of church history don't seem to work any longer. What we need now is a new set of tools. We need a new vision of reality, a new paradigm—a fundamental change in our thinking that leads to a fundamental change in our behavior, especially as it relates to our understanding of the church and mission.

That brings me to this book by Justin Wester. I love that Justin begins with the theological "why" of rethinking the nature of the church. He helps the reader understand the church as a people *called* and *sent* by God to participate in His redemptive mission. He challenges us to see that the nature of the church—rooted in the very nature of God—is missionary. Rather than seeing ourselves primarily as a *sending* body, we must see ourselves as a body that is *sent*.

But not only does Justin provide the needed imagination for rethinking mission—that focuses on the missionary habits of Jesus—but he challenges all of us to see ourselves as missionaries sent into the places we live, work and play. Presenting the "S.E.N.T." habits, Justin gives the reader an extremely practical tool for engaging their local context. If you desire to see genuine and long-lasting community impact, read what he suggests and step into the adventure with both feet.

Brad Brisco – Director of Bi-vocational Church Planting for the North American Mission Board and author of *The Missional Quest* and *Next Door as It Is in Heaven*

PART I
FOUNDATIONS
FOR LIVING S.E.N.T.

Chapter 1

YOU ARE S.E.N.T.

"As the Father has sent me, even so I am sending you."

Jesus

"Regardless of how God decides to route our paychecks, whether through a business or through a church, we are all full-time, paid missionaries."

Caesar Kalinowski

The church in the West is having an identity crisis. And when I say "church," I am not referring to a building. I am not referring to a physical space with a street address or an event that occurs on a particular day of the week. What I have in mind goes beyond three to four songs, announcements, a sermon, and a closing song with a prayer. I'm picturing something that doesn't fit nicely within an hour on Sunday mornings. Would it surprise you to hear that when the Scriptures refer to the "church" they have something entirely different in mind?

Ask any person today, "What is the church?" and you will likely hear a variety of responses: "It's a place where people go to worship God." "It's a time when religious people come together to listen to a teaching, sing songs, and pray." "It's an event where spiritual things take place." "It's a building on the street corner."

Can you blame them? This is how the majority of Christians are taught to think and talk about the church. From my earliest years I can remember getting ready to "go to church" by putting on my nicest clothes and combing my hair, rushing out the door, and jumping in the car so we wouldn't be "late for church," and upon my arrival being shown a nursery rhyme that reinforced these ideas. Remember this one?

> *Here's the church.*
> *Here's the steeple.*
> *Open the doors and see all the people.*
> *Here's the parson going upstairs.*
> *And here he is saying his prayers.*

As children interlock their fingers and fold their hands, the shape of a building emerges. Thumbs are set side-by-side to resemble a set of doors, and index fingers are sent skyward to fashion the unmistakable steeple. A simple online search for this nursery rhyme will bring up a popular website that explains how to lead this exercise with young children. Ironically, it is titled, "How to Create a Church with Your Fingers."

Behold—the church.

Is it any wonder then that most of us grow up believing the church is some combination of a place, time, or event? If it's not any of those things, then what exactly is *church*?

THE BUILDING BEHIND THE CHURCH

"Do you see the building behind the church?" That was the question that changed things for me. While sitting in class, a seminary professor projected an image onto the front screen. There was nothing unusual about it. It looked as if a congregation (maybe sixty to seventy people) had just concluded their service and decided to take a group picture in front of their church. That's when my professor asked, "Do you see the building behind the church?"

I looked behind the church, but all I could see were trees and shrubbery. Then I scanned the tree line. Nothing. After a few minutes of silence, my professor said, "Look closer." I squinted my eyes and checked the four corners of the photograph. Still no building. "Where is this thing?" I began to wonder. I looked around the class to see if my fellow students were struggling to find it like me. I couldn't tell, so I did the only thing I knew how—stare straight forward and pretend like I wasn't completely clueless.

Then my professor broke the silence. "Who sees it?" he asked. A few hands went up. He called on one and the student said, "It's right there." He said it as if my professor had just asked the dumbest of questions. I looked again at the picture as my professor walked to the screen at the front of the classroom. "Here is the building," my professor said, pointing to the church, "and here is the church," pointing to the people.

Ouch. Class dismissed.

The problem with thinking that the church is a place, time, or event is twofold. First, the Bible only refers to the church as *people*. The word we translate as "church" comes from the Greek word *ekklēsia* and simply means "a gathering or assembly of people." After Peter confesses Jesus to be the Christ in the Gospels, Jesus says, "And I tell you, you are Peter, and on this rock I will build my church, and the gates of hell shall not prevail against it."[1] Jesus was not referring to a building but to people. The first time the word "church" is used in the book of Acts it says, "And great fear came upon the whole church and upon all who heard of these things"—people.[2] Many of the apostle Paul's New Testament letters are addressed to churches, and in every case, to whom do you think he is directly writing? You guessed it—people. Whenever the church is mentioned in the Bible, it is always in relation to the redeemed people of God. If you are a Christ follower, then the church is who you are!

The second reason why referring to the church as a place, time, or event is problematic is because of the disempowering culture it creates. For example, referring to the church as a place often sounds like this: "Our church is the big one on the street corner," and "Are you ready to go to church?" Referring to the church as a time can sound like this: "Church starts at ten in the morning. Don't be late!" and "Church only happens on Sundays." When we speak in such a way, we are communicating that "church" is something other than people; in other words, that *we are not the*

---

[1] Matthew 16:18

[2] Acts 5:11

church. Unfortunately, this has gone on for far too long and has created a culture in which people believe that the church is not who they are but rather what they do for an hour every Sunday morning.

Would you speak about your family in the same way? How do each of these statements sound? (It may be helpful to read them aloud.)

"Our [family] is the big one on the street corner."

"Are you ready to go to [family]?"

"[Family] starts at ten in the morning. Don't be late!"

"[Family] only happens on Sundays."

Would we speak about our biological families in this way? Of course not! It sounds ridiculous. But many Christ followers (myself included!) are guilty of speaking about their church family in this way. Just like family is not what we do but who we are, church is not what we do but who we are.

WHO IS THE MISSIONARY, REALLY?

If someone said to you, "Please raise your hand if you are a Christ follower," would you raise it? I believe the majority of those reading this book would, in fact, raise their hands. But what if someone then said this to you: "Please keep your hand raised if you are a full-time missionary"? Would you keep your hand high in the air, or would you put it down? While standing before a classroom of roughly 200 students, I saw the answers to these questions play out before my eyes. After the former question was asked (to an evangelism class at a Christian university, I might add), most of the students raised their hands in agreement. However, when the latter question was asked, almost everyone's hand dropped.

Would it surprise you to hear that if you call yourself a Christ follower, then you are undoubtedly called to be a missionary? Sure, not everyone will be led by God to travel overseas, learn a new language, and dive headfirst into a foreign culture, but the same missionary identity is present in every Christ follower. Your particular calling may not be to cross the ocean; it may be to cross the street, to live like a missionary within your neighborhood, workplace, or community. The Scriptures make no distinction between your identity as a Christ follower and your identity as a missionary. They are one and the same.

But calling yourself a missionary and living like one are two different things. Being a missionary is far more than simply inviting someone to a church service or brushing up on your evangelism skills. Jesus has sent his church out to do the hard, cross-cultural work of reaching others with the gospel. This means the church should step into the world, not ask the world to step into the "church." Brad Brisco writes: "If we fail to go to the people, then to encounter the gospel meaningfully, they must come to us. This is the inbuilt assumption of the attractional church, and it requires that the nonbeliever do the cross-cultural work to find Jesus, and not us! . . . When we ask them to come to us, we are in essence asking *them* to be the missionaries!"[3]

---

[3] Brad Brisco, *Rethink: 9 Paradigm Shifts for Activating the Church*, (SEND Institute: 2015), 16.

And when you think about it, doesn't Jesus perfectly model for the church what a missionary should be? In the incarnation of Jesus, we see the Savior of the world step into the messiness of the world, rather than demand the world come to him on his terms. Eugene Peterson's translation of Jesus's incarnation within the Gospel of John poignantly reads, "The Word became flesh and blood and moved into the neighborhood."[4] Jesus did the hard, cross-cultural work of "moving into the neighborhood" to bring the Good News of the kingdom of God to those who most desperately needed it. He has shown us what it means to be a missionary, and he's calling his church to be the same.

So raise your hand if you're a Christ follower.

And keep your hand raised if you are a missionary.

YOU ARE S.E.N.T.

What if the church really believed these things about itself? Instead of Christ followers just going to church, what if the whole church went to the world? Instead of hands dropping in disagreement with being a missionary, can you imagine a room in which every hand stayed up? God's plan for the church is not limited to megachurch pastors, religious professionals, or elite "super-Christians." It is for every member of his church to live as though they have been sent on mission with Jesus in everyday life. Jeff Vanderstelt writes, "If you have the Spirit of God, you are a missionary sent by Jesus to tell the world who he is and what he has done. . . . Everywhere you go, whatever you do, you

---

[4] John 1:14, MSG

are a missionary sent by Jesus to love like Jesus, overcome sin like Jesus, proclaim the gospel like Jesus, and see people's lives changed by the power of the Spirit that raised Jesus from the dead."[5] The remainder of this book is dedicated to helping you do just that. Applying these four missional habits (S.E.N.T. habits) will reorient your life around God's mission and help you live like a missionary wherever you are:

See People like Jesus

Eat with People like Jesus

Neighbor People like Jesus

Talk with People About Jesus

But before actually getting to these S.E.N.T. habits, it is vitally important that we understand why we get to live S.E.N.T. in the first place. I will warn you: the following chapter is a rather lengthy story. If you are already a Christ follower, you may be tempted to skip over it. Don't! Taking the time to read the next chapter will help everything that follows make much more sense. Living S.E.N.T. is not some random fad or isolated church emphasis but rather an intentional way to live as "sent ones" of God. It's a way to partner with Jesus in what he is doing in the world today. The following chapter is intended to connect some theological dots and foster some much-needed motivation to begin living like a missionary wherever you are. You don't *have* to do this; you *get* to!

---

[5] Jeff Vanderstelt, *Saturate: Being Disciples of Jesus in the Everyday Stuff of Life,* (Wheaton, IL: Crossway, 2015), 165.

QUESTIONS TO CONSIDER

1. How do you normally refer to the church? As a place, time, or event? Or something else? Have you ever considered what kind of culture you are creating when you talk about the church?

2. Be honest with yourself: Would you have put your hand down if someone asked you if you were a full-time missionary? Why do you think Christ followers generally don't see themselves as such? How are you like a missionary?

3. What do you hope to get out of this book and study? What questions would you like to be answered?

Chapter 2

MISSIONAL MOVEMENTS

"Every Christian is either a missionary or an imposter."

C.H. Spurgeon

"The church doesn't just send missionaries;
the church is the missionary."

Brad Brisco

Crack open a Bible and you will see that God's mission permeates almost every page. The following story is a synopsis of the entire Bible told through the lens of four "missional movements." The first movement begins with God's *missional family*, tracing the family of Abraham all the way through their exodus from Egypt. The missional family eventually grows into the *missional nation*, and in this section, focused attention is given to the development of Israel and how they lived out their God-given calling. Next, the story reveals the *missional Savior*, showcasing and celebrating the person and work of Jesus Christ as part of God's redemptive plan. The final movement culminates with the missional Savior commissioning the *missional church* to live

S.E.N.T. Connecting these four missional movements across the Scriptures helps the church embrace their calling and live like everyday missionaries.

FROM THE BEGINNING

Even as early as the book of Genesis, God can be seen authorizing, commissioning, and sending people to be agents of his redemptive mission in the world. After sin enters the biblical story in Genesis 3, humanity plummets in a vicious spiral of depravity, and things seem to progress from bad to worse with each passing generation. Adam and Eve disobey God by eating of the Tree of the Knowledge of Good and Evil. Cain commits the first murder by killing his brother Abel. Wickedness multiplies within the hearts and minds of mankind. The nations collaboratively defy the Lord in the construction of the Tower of Babel.[6] And on and on it goes. Despite all these things, God, in his great love, initiates a restorative plan to undo the problems of the first eleven chapters of Genesis.

By commissioning Abram (Abraham) in Genesis 12, God grants him the promise of a lifetime and details his strategy for restoring all of fallen creation:

> Go from your country and your kindred and your
> father's house to the land that I will show you. And
> I will make of you a great nation, and I will bless
> you and make your name great, so that you will be

---

[6] See Genesis 3, 4, 6, and 11.

a blessing. I will bless those who bless you, and him who dishonors you I will curse, and in you all the families of the earth shall be blessed.[7]

God's plan was to use this man to bring about his redemptive mission and thus "bless" all men. This chosen man and his offspring would be God's "missional family" on earth.

MISSIONAL FAMILY

In order for God's missional family to fulfill their calling, Abram first had to go. Abram had been commissioned by a sending God who called him to get up, pack up, and go—to gather his belongings, leave, and live in a foreign land. For what purpose? So that he, his family, and the nation that would eventually come from him (Israel) would bring about the blessing of God wherever they went.[8]

While the book of Genesis overviews God's redemption strategy through the missional family of Abraham, the book of Exodus details the implementation of that plan through the people of Israel. As the story of God continues to unfold, Abraham's missional family multiplies in number and is forced into slavery by a ruthless Egyptian pharaoh. As the Israelites' cries for deliverance reach the ears of God, the book of Exodus says, "God remembered his covenant with Abraham, with Isaac, and with

[7] Genesis 12:1-3

[8] The Lord affirms his covenant promise to both Isaac (26:4) and Jacob (28:14).

Jacob. God saw the people of Israel—and God knew."[9] Being motivated by his justice and his faithfulness to the covenant promises made to Abraham, God commissions Moses to help bring about redemption for Israel. What follows is the epic story of how God redeems the people of Israel from Egyptian bondage, calls them into a covenant relationship, and eventually dwells in their midst. And it is this event—the Exodus—that becomes the defining experience for this missional family.

The Exodus literally paves the way for the Israelites to journey to Mount Sinai, where they would receive the Law from God himself. It is in this Law where specific instructions are given about how this missional family was to live among the nations and fulfill their calling. Exodus 19:3-6 states:

> The LORD called to [Moses] out of the mountain, saying, "Thus you shall say to the house of Jacob, and tell the people of Israel: 'You yourselves have seen what I did to the Egyptians, and how I bore you on eagles' wings and brought you to myself. Now therefore, if you will indeed obey my voice and keep my covenant, you shall be my treasured possession among all peoples, for all the earth is mine; and you shall be to me a kingdom of priests and a holy nation.' These are the words that you shall speak to the people of Israel."[10]

---

[9] Exodus 2:24-25

[10] Exodus 19:3-6

They would demonstrate to the watching world what redemptive living looks like in real life and in real time. By passionately obeying the Law, their interactions with foreigners, sojourners, and aliens would display God's tangible blessing to the nations. God used the Exodus to shape the way this missional family interacted with and treated those in their midst:

- "You shall not wrong a sojourner or oppress him, for you were sojourners in the land of Egypt." (Exodus 22:21)

- "You shall not oppress a sojourner. You know the heart of a sojourner, for you were sojourners in the land of Egypt." (Exodus 23:9)

- "When a stranger sojourns with you in your land, you shall not do him wrong. You shall treat the stranger who sojourns with you as the native among you, and you shall love him as yourself, for you were strangers in the land of Egypt: I am the LORD your God." (Lev. 19:33-34)

- "He executes justice for the fatherless and the widow, and loves the sojourner, giving him food and clothing. Love the sojourner, therefore, for you were sojourners in the land of Egypt." (Deut. 10:18-19)

- "You shall not pervert the justice due to the sojourner or to the fatherless, or take a widow's garment in pledge, but you shall remember that you were a slave in Egypt and the LORD your God redeemed you from there; therefore I command you to do this." (Deut. 24:17-18)

It is through the lens of the Exodus that the Lord widens the scope of this missional family's compassion and care for the nations. As the people of Israel wander through the desert and eventually come to the Promised Land of Canaan, the next few books of the Old Testament (Joshua, Judges, 1 and 2 Samuel, and 1 and 2 Kings) describe how this missional family transitions into God's missional nation.

MISSIONAL NATION

The book of Joshua opens almost immediately with a snapshot of how God's redemptive mission continues to unfold throughout the Scriptures. While Israel prepares to invade the Promised Land, they send two spies into the city of Jericho on a reconnaissance mission. The spies wisely choose to hide out in the house of a pagan prostitute named Rahab. After the spies' whereabouts have been discovered by the king, Rahab hides the spies in her home and sends the king to look for them outside the city walls (a wild-goose chase for sure). In exchange for Rahab's kindness to the spies, the Israelites spare her family's household during the invasion. As time goes on, Rahab marries an Israelite and eventually becomes the mother of Boaz, the great-great-grandmother of King David, and is named within the genealogy of Jesus Christ in the Gospel of Matthew! In the midst of Israel's military conquests in Canaan, the story of Rahab highlights that God's promise to

Abraham extends well beyond cultural lines and that his salvation reaches to all who put their faith in him.

Under Joshua's leadership, the Israelites flourishes in their newly acquired territory. The story, however, takes a radical turn for the worse during the time after Joshua's death and the generations that follow. Israel failed to drive out all of the native inhabitants within the land of Canaan, and, as time went on, generations arose that didn't walk in the ways of the Lord. Early on, the book of Judges issues this statement: "And there arose another generation after them who did not know the LORD or the work that he had done for Israel."[11] Israel is plagued by their constant struggle with idolatry (worshipping foreign gods) and, ultimately, their failure to live up to their missional calling.

What follows is a period of time in which the Lord raised up several "judges" (military leaders) to deliver Israel from their surrounding enemies. Through each judge's military campaign, Israel would experience peace and rest. However, soon after the judge's death, Israel would turn back to its old ways, serving foreign gods and forsaking the way of the Lord. This back-and-forth cycle (Israel's sin, foreign oppression, Israel's repentance, Israel's deliverance) would likely cause you or me to "throw in the towel" on the whole plan, yet the Lord continues to preserve this people for his redemptive mission in the world.

In the book of 1 Samuel, God raises up a judge named Samuel who leads Israel back to the Lord and helps establish a more stable form of leadership for the nation. Samuel eventually anoints a

---

[11] Judges 2:10

young man named David as king over Israel to help nourish their missional calling. Just like Abraham in the book of Genesis, God establishes a covenant with David in the book of 2 Samuel:

> And I have been with you wherever you went and have cut off all your enemies from before you. And I will make for you a great name, like the name of the great ones of the earth. And I will appoint a place for my people Israel and will plant them, so that they may dwell in their own place and be disturbed no more. . . . When your days are fulfilled and you lie down with your fathers, I will raise up your offspring after you, who shall come from your body, and I will establish his kingdom. He shall build a house for my name, and I will establish the throne of his kingdom forever. I will be to him a father, and he shall be to me a son.[12]

Not only does this covenant with David help fulfill the covenant made with Abraham, it also anticipates the final goal of God's redemptive work—the blessing of all nations through Israel. This chosen nation and its inhabitants would be God's missional nation on earth.

As Israel witnesses the succession of kings over the years, some prove to be faithful. But, by and large, the majority of the kings utterly fail. These kings fail to meet the spiritual and ethical

---

[12] 2 Samuel 7:9-10, 12-14

standards placed upon them, and the nation as a whole largely mirrors their unfaithfulness. Yet again, God does not give up on his missional nation and decides to send a series of prophets, or "covenant keepers," to bring his people back to himself and remind them of their calling.

Unfortunately, the nation does not heed the prophets' words nor repent of their unfaithfulness to God and is subsequently warned of an impending judgment (exile). Something drastic has to occur to restore God's missional nation to who they were meant to be and what they were called to do. Christopher Wright explains, "God's mission to the nations is being hindered because of Israel's continuing spiritual and ethical failure. Let Israel return to *their* mission (to be the people of YHWH, worshipping him exclusively and living according to his moral demands), and God can return to *his* mission—blessing the nations."[13]

Finally, when God has had enough, he sends in two national superpowers (Assyria and Babylon) to carry out his judgment, and by 586 BC the entire missional nation has been scattered into exile.[14] No more national prominence. No more national autonomy. Is this the end? What role could an exile possibly play in carrying out God's redemptive mission in the world? Interestingly, much like the Exodus was for the missional family, it is this

---

[13] Christopher Wright, *The Mission of God's People*, (Grand Rapids, MI: Zondervan, 2010), 241.

[14] Prior to the Exile, the nation of Israel splits into two kingdoms: the northern kingdom called "Israel" and the southern kingdom referred to as "Judah." In 722 BC, the northern kingdom is scattered by the Assyrians. In 586 BC, the southern kingdom is scattered by the Babylonians.

event—namely, the Exile—that becomes the defining experience for God's missional nation.

During the Exile, Israel's perspective about their relationship with their foreign oppressors changes. Rather than withdraw into isolation, the Lord calls them to bless the Babylonian empire by fully engaging in the cultural life of the empire. The prophet Jeremiah writes:

> Thus says the LORD of hosts, the God of Israel, to all the exiles whom I have sent into exile from Jerusalem to Babylon: Build houses and live in them; plant gardens and eat their produce. Take wives and have sons and daughters; take wives for your sons, and give your daughters in marriage, that they may bear sons and daughters; multiply there, and do not decrease. But seek the welfare of the city where I have sent you into exile, and pray to the LORD on its behalf, for in its welfare you will find your welfare.[15]

Through the lens of the Exile, Israel is reminded of their purpose as God's missional nation. Their current state of exile was not to be wasted by withdrawing into isolation or blindly assimilating into the surrounding culture. Rather, they were being *trained* in exile to preserve their identity and calling by living lives passionately devoted to God. In exile and even after, Israel

---

[15] Jeremiah 29:4-7

would be used by God to extend his blessing to the entire world. Here is how the prophet Isaiah states that Israel will do so:

- "I am the LORD; I have called you in righteousness;
    I will take you by the hand and keep you;
  I will give you as a covenant for the people,
    a light for the nations," (Isaiah 42:6)

- "It is too light a thing that you should be my servant
    to raise up the tribes of Jacob
    and to bring back the preserved of Israel;
  I will make you as a light for the nations,
    that my salvation may reach to the end of the earth."
  (Isaiah 49:6)

- "The LORD has bared his holy arm
    before the eyes of all the nations,
  and all the ends of the earth shall see
    the salvation of our God." (Isaiah 52:10)

- "And nations shall come to your light,
    and kings to the brightness of your rising." (Isaiah 60:3)

Allen Hilton writes, "The lamp of the people of Israel shall shine again, and this time it will not be a private viewing. Israel will be a blessing to all the families of the earth. God's prophets did not speak that way before the people had been trained by exile."[16]

---

[16] Allen Hilton, "Living into the Big Story: The Missional Trajectory of Scripture in Congregational Life," in *Cultivating Sent Communities*, ed. Dwight J. Zscheile, (Grand Rapids, MI: Eerdman's, 2012), 93.

Through much of the Old Testament, we catch glimpses of God's mission being carried out through God's people. But for the most part, Israel struggles to live up to their calling to be a blessing to the nations. Time and time again, the Lord sends his agents (Moses, the judges, the Davidic kings, and the prophets) to realign Israel's disobedient trajectory. Their failure to walk in his ways and their perpetual unfaithfulness prompt the Lord to exercise judgment on his beloved covenant people. Israel would need a complete "do-over" if they were to be successful in fulfilling their calling. Thankfully, that is exactly what God has in mind, though it's not anywhere close to what Israel expected. All of the previous failings of Israel would be corrected and completed in the "missional Savior," Jesus Christ.

MISSIONAL SAVIOR

After roughly 400 years of agonizing silence, the New Testament opens with great news: the announcement of the birth of Jesus. Why is this such great news? As Christopher Wright states, "Jesus did not just arrive; he was sent."[17] He was sent by God the Father for a specific reason and to fulfill a specific purpose. In fact, both Mary, the mother of Jesus, and Zechariah, the father of John the Baptist, recognize the birth of Jesus as the fulfillment of the original redemptive promises made to Abraham. Mary said:

---

[17] Christopher Wright, *The Mission of God's People*, (Grand Rapids, MI: Zondervan, 2010), 210.

"My soul magnifies the Lord,
    and my spirit rejoices in God my Savior,
for he has looked on the humble estate of his servant.
    For behold, from now on all generations will call me
blessed;
for he who is mighty has done great things for me,
    and holy is his name.
And his mercy is for those who fear him
    from generation to generation.
He has shown strength with his arm;
    he has scattered the proud in the thoughts of their hearts;
he has brought down the mighty from their thrones
    and exalted those of humble estate;
he has filled the hungry with good things,
    and the rich he has sent away empty.
He has helped his servant Israel,
    in remembrance of his mercy,
as he spoke to our fathers,
    to Abraham and to his offspring forever."[18]

Zechariah said:

"Blessed be the Lord God of Israel,
    for he has visited and redeemed his people
and has raised up a horn of salvation for us
    in the house of his servant David,
as he spoke by the mouth of his holy prophets from of old,
    that we should be saved from our enemies
    and from the hand of all who hate us;

---

[18] Luke 1:46-55

to show the mercy promised to our fathers
    and to remember his holy covenant,
the oath that he swore to our father Abraham, to grant us
that we, being delivered from the hand of our enemies,
might serve him without fear,
    in holiness and righteousness before him all our days."[19]

Why is this important? The progression from missional family to missional nation to missional Savior is not a series of unrelated events. These movements are inseparably connected and paint a beautiful and cohesive picture of how God has been working to fulfill his mission in the world. In many ways, Jesus's life and ministry is a retelling of the story of Israel, but where the missional nation failed, the missional Savior succeeded.

Through the entirety of Jesus's ministry, he lives out the reality that he has been "sent" by the Father to accomplish his redemptive mission. This can be most clearly seen within the Gospel of John (emphasis added):

- "Jesus said to them, 'My food is to do the will of him who **sent** me and to accomplish his work.' " (John 4:34)

- "I can do nothing on my own. As I hear, I judge, and my judgment is just, because I seek not my own will but the will of him who **sent** me." (John 5:30)

---

[19] Luke 1:68-75

- "Jesus answered them, 'This is the work of God, that you believe in him whom he has **sent**.' " (John 6:29)

- "Jesus said to them, 'If God were your Father, you would love me, for I came from God and I am here. I came not of my own accord, but he **sent** me.'" (John 8:42)

- "We must work the works of him who **sent** me while it is day; night is coming, when no one can work." (John 9:4)

- "Truly, truly, I say to you, whoever receives the one I send receives me, and whoever receives me receives the one who **sent** me." (John 13:20)

- "As you **sent** me into the world, so I have **sent** them into the world." (John 17:18)

- "Jesus said to them again, 'Peace be with you. As the Father has **sent** me, even so I am **sending** you.'" (John 20:21)

Jesus is sent to preach the good news of the kingdom of God and, in so doing, begins to gather people together who are called to be a part of the kingdom movement. However, this kingdom would not be like the one experienced by the missional nation in the Old Testament. Halter and Smay explain:

> He calls God's reign "the kingdom" and says that it is now at hand. But there is a twist to his message. God's heavenly rule and his deliverance are

not going to come in the form of military con-
quest over Rome, another exodus from slavery to
a foreign nation (as many expected). The kingdom
will penetrate the slavery of sin and set human
hearts free to live out the life that Jesus taught and
demonstrated.[20]

Jesus's entire life was submitted to the will of his Father and was
laser focused on finishing the work he had been sent to do. This
work culminates at the cross, where the curse of sin was paid for
with his blood and provision for salvation was made by his death.
With the authoritative words, "It is finished!" Jesus bowed his head,
breathed his last, and gave up his spirit.[21] God's plan of redemption
was complete. But the story was far from over.

After three days, Jesus is miraculously raised back to life, and
his disciples can hardly believe it! He now explains that his disciples would carry on this redemptive mission in all of the world by
sharing the good news of the kingdom of God with anyone and
everyone. He says in John 20, "Peace be with you. As the Father
has sent me, even so I am sending you."[22] He was sending his
followers out to make disciples of all the nations. The missional
Savior was sending and commissioning his "missional church"!

---

[20] Halter and Smay, *AND: The Gathered and Scattered Church*, (Grand
Rapids, MI: Zondervan, 2010), 43.

[21] John 19:30

[22] John 20:21

MISSIONAL CHURCH

Before Jesus ascends into heaven, he tells his small, hodgepodge group of followers this: "But you will receive power when the Holy Spirit has come upon you, and you will be my witnesses in Jerusalem and in all Judea and Samaria, and to the end of the earth."[23] What an incredibly huge vision and calling! The rest of the book of Acts details how the early church was led in fulfilling that vision from the city of Jerusalem all the way to the heart of the Gentile world, the city of Rome. The early church was a missional church, sent out by Jesus in the power of the Holy Spirit to join God in his redemptive mission. Wright explains:

> From Jesus, then, flows the mission of the church until he comes again. His final words to his disciples and action form a sending, a commission, a mandate. Those who are disciples of Jesus today are to be like the disciples of Jesus in the Gospels— called to be with him and to go in his name to do his work, to the ends of the earth and until the end of the world. Churches, then, are to be communities around the world, planted, nurtured, and connected through ministries of sending, going, and supporting—for the sake of the name of Christ and the truth of the gospel.[24]

---

[23] Acts 1:8

[24] Christopher Wright, *The Mission of God's People*, (Grand Rapids, MI: Zondervan, 2010), 221.

YOU HAVE BEEN SENT

So, what does this have to do with you and your local church? Everything! If you are a follower of Christ, that means you—and everyone in your local church—is a full-time minister of the gospel who has been commissioned by Jesus to live a "sent" life. And if you really think about it, that changes everything. It changes how we gather as the church. It changes how we scatter as the church. It means that we need to interpret our neighborhoods, workplaces, and cities as places to which we have been sent. It means that we need to interpret our social networks, neighbors, and communities as people to whom we have been sent. We don't *have* to do this. We *get* to do this!

Be honest. Is this how you see yourself? Do you see yourself as a missionary? As one who has been sent? When you survey the missional movements of Scripture (missional family, missional nation, missional Savior, missional church), does something in your heart come alive? The church was designed for this. You are called to this, and the reality is this: you are sent. Every follower of Christ has been sent by Jesus into the world to join him in mission.

Answering the question of how we do this is the focus of the remainder of this book. In what follows, I will propose a helpful acronym around the word *sent,* where each letter represents a different "missional habit." These habits are simple, scalable, and reproducible and—when practiced with gospel intentionality—help activate everyone to live as everyday, ordinary missionaries.

QUESTIONS TO CONSIDER

1. Which of the four missional movements within Scripture (missional family, missional nation, missional Savior, missional Church) was most helpful in seeing the bigger story of God's mission throughout history?

2. How do you respond to what C.H. Spurgeon said at the beginning of the chapter ("Every Christian is either a missionary or an imposter.")? Do you agree with this? Why or why not?

3. If you began to see yourself as a missionary sent by Jesus, how would this change the way you interacted with your family, friends, neighbors, coworkers, or classmates?

Chapter 3

S.E.N.T. HABITS

"We cannot continue to try to think our way into a new
way of acting, but rather we need to act our way into a new
way of thinking."

Alan Hirsch

All of us have habits. You may not think you do, but trust me, you
do. Some of our ingrained habits may be very healthy and admirable, but others may be just the opposite. From the moment we
wake up in the morning until the moment we go to sleep at night,
all of us operate out of the habits we have consciously created or
inadvertently adopted. In fact, the American philosopher Will
Durant, in summarizing many of Aristotle's teachings, stated,
"We are what we repeatedly do."[25] Our everyday lives, therefore,
are the combination of a series of learned habits developed over
years and years of practice.

Our day-to-day routines are filled with all kinds of habits that
seem to let us run on autopilot, almost acting without thinking.

---

[25] Will Durant, *The Story of Philosophy*, (New York, NY: Simon and Schuster,
1961), 98.

The most obvious of these is driving. Think back to when you were younger, first learning to drive, and preparing to get your learner's permit. Our brains were under an enormous workload: Seatbelt on. Adjust the seat. Adjust side and rearview mirrors. Key in the ignition. Foot on the brake to put vehicle into drive. Look both ways before pulling out of the driveway. Gas on the right. Brake on the left (but use your right foot because you may need your left foot when driving a car with a manual transmission!). Turn signal before changing lanes. And on and on it went. But for those who have been driving for years, many of these practices have become routine—so routine that we sometimes perform them without conscious effort.

Have you ever gotten into your car, driven home, and when you pulled into your driveway realized you have no recollection of your commute? Whether we were preoccupied by other stimuli (on an important phone call, having a meaningful conversation with a passenger, jamming out to a favorite tune) or lost in deep reflection, the result is the same: we have so ingrained the habits of driving into our lives that we often perform them without thinking. The development of these habits took quite a bit of mental energy on the front end, but as we practiced them over and over, these habits entrenched themselves into our lives and now require much less attention. And it is the same with learning a new set of habits: S.E.N.T. habits.

This new set of habits can change the way we live throughout the week, not just on Sundays. If Jesus has sent you on mission (and he has!), then he expects that we will engage in that mission for the remainder of our lives. These habits, when practiced with intentionality, help to propel each of us into the world around us. They will likely take an enormous amount of mental energy and effort on the front end, but, with repeated practice, they can become almost second nature. Remember the driving analogy? Let's bring in a "learner's permit" level of purposefulness in cultivating these habits until they become a part of who we are. Now you may be wondering: "What exactly are these habits? Where did they come from? And what does each of them mean?"

JESUS LIVED S.E.N.T.

Four habits can be derived from the life and ministry of Jesus Christ found in the four Gospels. While far from comprehensive, these habits routinely show up in the way he lived his life. Jesus practiced these four habits flawlessly and, in so doing, perfectly fulfilled the mission for which he was sent. You and I, likewise, can emulate these S.E.N.T. habits and respond to God's invitation to join his mission in the world. Here are the four habits:

See People like Jesus

- Jesus had an uncanny ability to pick people out of a crowd. In Mark 5, a woman pushes through a crowd to touch Jesus's clothing, and he notices her amid the numerous other people bumping into him. In Luke 7, a funeral procession is making its way through the town of Nain, and Jesus spots the mother of the deceased, a widow, and raises her son back to life. And in Luke 19, upon entering the town of Jericho, Jesus looks up and spots a small-statured man sitting in a tree. As Jesus passes through the crowd, he speaks to the man and lodges at his house for the night. Time and time again, Jesus takes note of others, treats them with grace and respect, and sees them for who they really are.

Eat with People like Jesus

- Jesus leveraged the meal time to do some of his most incredible work, teach some of his most profound truths, and train some of his most committed followers. Soon after calling a tax collector named Levi to be one of his disciples in Mark 2, Jesus is seen at a party with the local riffraff. It's during this meal that he says, "I came not to call the righteous, but sinners." During a meal at a prominent Pharisee's house, Jesus publicly forgave the sins of a prostitute (Luke 7:48). During a meal at a chief tax collector's house, Jesus said, "The Son of Man came to seek and to save the lost" (Luke 19:10). During a Passover meal, Jesus instituted the Lord's Supper (Luke 22:14). And *only* over a meal did the disciples on the road to Emmaus recognize the risen Christ (Luke 24:30-31)! Jesus's intentionality around the shared meal was instrumental in carrying out his ministry.

Neighbor People like Jesus

- When asked by a lawyer which commandment in the Law was the greatest, Jesus responded, "You shall love the Lord your God with all your heart and with all your soul and with all your mind. This is the great and first commandment. And a second is like it: You shall love your neighbor as yourself. On these two commandments depend all the Law and the Prophets."[26] Think about that for a second. *All* of the Old Testament Law and Prophets depend on those *two* commandments! Jesus didn't just point this out so we would love our neighbor in an ambiguous, metaphorical way. No, Jesus quite literally loved his neighbor as himself and expects each of his followers to do the same.

Talk with People About Jesus

- As Jesus began his ministry, he quoted the prophet Isaiah in a synagogue in the town of Nazareth: "The Spirit of the Lord is upon me, because he has anointed me to proclaim good news to the poor. He has sent me to proclaim liberty to the captives and recovering of sight to the blind, to set at liberty those who are oppressed, to proclaim the year of the Lord's favor."[27] Jesus had a message to bring—

---

[26] Matthew 22:37-40

[27] Luke 4:18-19

not a message of condemnation, but one of good
news. We, in turn, get to be witnesses to this good
news and help alert people to the reign of Christ!

Okay, I know what you're thinking: "Those S.E.N.T. habits are
great for Jesus, but I am not Jesus!" You're right. You aren't. But
he has promised to be *with you* as you live S.E.N.T. and make
disciples. You are not responsible for the results of these habits,
but you are responsible for obedience to his commands in the
Scriptures. And living S.E.N.T. can help you do just that.

YOU CAN LIVE S.E.N.T.

Let's face it. All of us have a natural, habitual way of seeing other
people, eating, being a neighbor, and talking with others about
our faith. For some, your natural, habitual way of seeing people
may be to ignore them, to quickly look away so as not to make eye
contact, or to remain so preoccupied in your day that you have
no time for others. Are we seeing other people as Jesus would,
or have we reduced others to interruptions and annoyances? For
some, your ingrained habit of eating may be to eat alone, scarf
down your food in a hurry, and return to work. Are we eating
like Jesus or are we eating like fast-food-crazed Americans? For
some, your habitual way of being a neighbor is to retreat into the
comfort and safety of your home, mind your own business, and
keep interactions with neighbors to a minimum. Are we interacting with our neighbors like Jesus would have, or have we become
suburbanized? For some, your default way of talking to others

about your faith is simply to never bring it up, deeming the topic too personal and private to discuss. Are we talking to others as Jesus would, or do we succumb to fear?

In whatever measure these practices already exist in your life, the good news is this: you can change. In fact, the gospel challenges every one of us to change. It challenges us to change in our whole lives, not just in a component or section of them. Thus the entirety of our lives, not just one day of the week, is a reflection of our faith in Christ (how we invest our time, how we interact with and relate to others, how we manage our possessions, how we conduct ourselves in our vocations, how we choose to raise our children). If our only "Christian" habits are going to church services on Sundays and saying "grace" before meals, how will the world come to know the Good News of the gospel? Mike Frost elaborates, "If our only habits as Christians are going to church and attending meetings, they're not going to connect us with unbelievers nor invite their curiosity about our faith."[28] We need a new set of missional habits that propel us outward, helping us to be the Good News people we were meant to be.

SEE. EAT. NEIGHBOR. TALK.

I will explain more about each of these habits in the chapters to come, but for now, here is a brief summary of the habits and the measures associated with each:

[28] Mike Frost, *Surprise the World*, (Colorado Springs, CO: NavPress), 21-22.

See People like Jesus	*Meet three new people this week, one of whom is not a member of my church.*
Eat with People like Jesus	*Eat with three people this week, one of whom is not a member of my church.*
Neighbor People like Jesus	*Take one next step with a literal neighbor this week.*
Talk with People About Jesus	*Have one gospel conversation this week.*

By "See People like Jesus," I mean to say that we should prioritize making at least three meaningful connections with others in a week's time. One of those connections needs to be with someone who is not a member or attender of your local church. This person could be a neighbor, a coworker, a friend of a friend, or a complete stranger. I should mention that all the S.E.N.T. habits rely upon and work with one another, but "See People like Jesus" is certainly the first step to the entire process.

"Eat with People like Jesus" is really about developing and deepening relationships with others by opening up your life. One of the best places to cultivate this habit is within your own home, but it doesn't have to be there. This habit is designed to foster intentional hospitality, whether that be in your home or else-where. Strive to share three intentional meals in a week's time, one of which needs to be with a person not affiliated with your local church.

By "Neighbor People like Jesus," I mean to focus on your lit-eral neighbors. Our literal neighbors are so important because they are the ones in our immediate sphere of influence and, sadly, the ones we most often neglect. The goal is to take one "next step" with a literal neighbor in a week's time. We will go into more detail about what is meant by "next steps," but suffice it to say it could have a wide range of applications, from learning your neighbors' names to having them over for dinner to looking for ways to serve them throughout the week.

"Talk with People About Jesus" is just like it sounds: talking with other people about the gospel, your faith, and the kingdom of God. This practice may be more refreshing to your ears than you think. This habit seeks to foster gospel fluency in your every-day speech by having open-ended conversations with others as opposed to the traditional approach of "gospel presentations." We will talk more about the difference between the two in later chapters, but for now it's just important to understand the gist: have one "gospel conversation" within a week's time.

S.E.N.T. POTENTIAL

In the moment, many of these S.E.N.T. habits may not feel significant or produce dramatic, overnight results. However, these subtle rhythms, over time, can yield some amazing things.

Darren Hardy wrote a small yet profound book in 2010 called *The Compound Effect*. One of its chief principles is found in the following equation:

**Small, Smart Choices + Consistency + Time =
RADICAL DIFFERENCE**[29]

In one of his examples, Hardy presents two options: take $3 million in cash *right now* or take one penny that doubles every day for the next thirty-one days. It's tempting to take the cold hard cash up front, but using his compound effect formula, that would be the wrong choice! Interestingly, the person who chose the penny would lag behind the person who took the up-front cash until day thirty of the thirty-one-day race. On that day, the "penny choice" would actually surpass the three million dollars, and by the last day (day thirty-one), the person who chose the penny would end up with $10,737,418.24! Sometimes it's prudent to pull back and consider the bigger picture. Sometimes we need to pause and consider something's potential.

The following figure estimates the reach of the S.E.N.T. habits in a year's time. Additionally, the numbers have been calculated to reflect the results of one person living a S.E.N.T. life, three people doing so, and also a local church of a hundred people.

Can you imagine cultivating meaningful relationships with 156 people in a year? Having 156 meals fueled by gospel intentionality? Taking fifty-two "next steps" with your closest

---

[29] Darren Hardy, *The Compound Effect*, (Boston, MA: Da Capo Press, 2010), 10.

S.E.N.T. Habit	You	Three People	A Church of 100
See People like Jesus	156 people	468 people	15,600 people
Eat with People like Jesus	156 meals	468 meals	15,600 meals
Neighbor People like Jesus	52 next steps	156 next steps	5,200 next steps
Talk with People About Jesus	52 gospel conversations	156 gospel conversations	5,200 gospel conversations

neighbors? Having fifty-two gospel conversations? How about a local church that purposefully connects with 15,600 nonmembers in a year? Shares more than 15,000 gospel-saturated meals with others, loves their community in thousands of tangible ways, and shares the Good News thousands and thousands of times a year? Just the idea of a person, a small group, or a local church living S.E.N.T. for one year could change entire households, neighborhoods, and cities with the gospel! What are you waiting for? Let's live S.E.N.T.

QUESTIONS TO CONSIDER

1. A few examples were given of Jesus living S.E.N.T. What other examples come to mind? (Try to find at least one example for each habit from the Gospels.)

2. As you think about changing some of your habits, which of the S.E.N.T. habits will be easiest to adopt? Most difficult?

3. Challenge: Conduct a weekly audit by focusing on the S.E.N.T. habits. Which ones do you naturally do? Which ones do you naturally avoid?

PART II
MISSIONAL HABITS

Chapter 4

SEE PEOPLE LIKE JESUS

"The Samaritan woman said to him, 'How is it that you, a
Jew, ask for a drink from me, a woman of Samaria?'"

John 4:9

I have a small poster in my office of two people in front of a corner store. It's late. It's raining, and it looks like there could be a
slight chill in the air. Trash is all over the ground. Signs for cheap
beer and cigarettes cover the plate-glass windows behind them.
One of them, presumably the boyfriend, is using a pay phone
(remember those?) to make a call while his pregnant girlfriend
is sitting on top of a broken, coin-operated amusement ride for
kids. At first glance, the poster scene is fairly ordinary.

Then, just as you begin to walk away, something catches your
eye. Maybe it's the name of the girl's high school printed on her
hoodie ("Nazareth High School"). Or maybe you realize that the
boyfriend is calling motels because the one behind him ("Dave's
City Motel") has no vacancies. Then you realize you have a
strange feeling of familiarity with this scene. The cigarette poster
wants you to smoke "Wiseman Cigarettes." The fluorescent beer
sign says "Star Beer." The graffiti on the side of the phone booth

José y Maria, Everett Patterson

reads "Ezek 34:15-16," and the newspaper on the ground has an ad on the front page for "Shepherd Watches." Maybe this poster is special after all.

Originally designed to be a Christmas card, this poster was created by Everett Patterson, an artist in Portland, Oregon, to depict the parents of Jesus in a modern-day setting.

For me, though, it's a great deal more than a Christmas card. I realize that I have encountered people like this before, possibly even seeing and passing them by every single day. They are people who don't look like me, dress like me, or even talk like me but who are nonetheless image-bearers of God. They are individuals who possess inherent worth and have unique stories of their own. They are people who I, at best, unintentionally overlook and, at worst, intentionally ignore as I go about my day-to-day routine. All too often, these individuals are reduced to nothing more than a category in my mind, making it that much easier to pass them by.

INDIVIDUALS NOT CATEGORIES

In Jesus's day, certain people, places, and politics simply did not mix. Good Jews wouldn't travel through Samaria. Good Jews wouldn't touch lepers. Good Jews wouldn't eat with, let alone party with, tax collectors and sinners. In the first century, people were categorized by economic status and deeply held religious convictions (sounds a lot like today, huh?), making it crystal clear to which group and subgroup persons and families belonged. Intentionally crossing one of these cultural categories certainly raised more than a few eyebrows and had the potential to destroy a reputation and earn you a nasty social stigma. I presume the interaction process was a lot like it is today: When you see a person, you determine if they are in your preferred category. If the answer is yes, then by all means interact with them. If the answer is no, don't even bother. In fact, it's probably best just to steer clear of them.

In *Disunity in Christ*, Christina Cleveland sheds light on our natural tendency to distance ourselves from, or altogether avoid, certain categories of people. She suggests that within a split second of time, we have the capacity to categorize people into one of two groups: those "like us" or those "unlike us" (often termed *ingroup* and *outgroup*).[30] While not all categorization is bad, classifying human beings this way certainly influences the way we interact with and treat them. We can take in the color of a person's skin, the clothing they wear, the way they speak, and a multitude of other split-second social cues and make a judgment call about whether that person is "in" or "out." If they are determined to be part of our ingroup, favorable opinions and interactions usually follow. If they fall within our outgroup, the opposite can be true. The unintended result of this type of thinking is that people are stripped of their individuality and are reduced to being nothing more than a category, which makes it that much easier for us to disregard them entirely. So why does Jesus, time and time again, willingly cross these categories and interact with the marginalized and the outcast? What does he see in others that most of us do not?

PIT STOP IN SAMARIA

In chapter 4 of the Gospel of John, Jesus consciously breaks through three distinct categories to get to the individual. The first category is the category of *place*. Jesus and his disciples set out on a journey from Judea to Galilee. Instead of taking the customary detour, which would have avoided the region of Samaria, Jesus

---

30 Christina Cleveland, *Disunity in Christ,* (Downers Grove, IL: IVP Books, 2013), 49.

insists on the shorter route and ends up in a Samaritan town called Sychar. This was a really big deal. Jews and Samaritans had a long history of hostility toward one another, and their categorization of one another had festered into a deeply rooted animosity. Yet Jesus *chose* to travel through this region. Chuck Swindoll writes, "To [Jews], Samaritans were idolatrous half-breeds—ethnically polluted, religiously confused, and morally debased."[31] I'm sure the twelve disciples weren't too thrilled about Jesus's travel plan, even if it did mean a shorter trip for them.

Tired from the journey, Jesus sits down next to a well just as a Samaritan woman approaches to draw water for herself. Here is where Jesus crosses the second category—the category of *people*. Since the biblical story doesn't mention anyone else around, it would seem that Jesus and the woman are alone when the unexpected happens. Jesus, a Jewish man, intentionally engages a Samaritan woman in conversation! That may not come as a surprise to you and me, as we tend to read this passage from a twenty-first century Western perspective, but it certainly shocked the woman. She asks him, "How is it that you, a Jew, ask for a drink from me, a woman of Samaria?" Since he has no bucket to draw water with, Jesus seems to be insinuating that they would be sharing the same cup (imagine ordering a drink for two people with only one straw!). Even Jesus's own disciples were astounded to find him speaking to her when they arrive on the scene. Verse 27 states (emphasis added): "Just then his disciples came back. They *marveled* that he was talking with a

---

[31] Chuck Swindoll, *Swindoll's New Testament Insights,* (Grand Rapids, MI: Zondervan, 2010), 85.

woman, but no one said, 'What do you seek?' or, 'Why are you talking with *her*?'" It would seem that Jesus's actions were not as admirable as they were questionable.

The final category that Jesus intentionally crosses is the category of *persuasion*. He knew that this woman would have a completely different set of beliefs than he did, but that did not stop him from engaging and discussing them with her. He knew that her lifestyle choices were different than his: "You are right in saying, 'I have no husband'; for you have had five husbands, and the one you now have is not your husband."[32] He knew that her spiritual beliefs were different than his: "You worship what you do not know; we worship what we know, for salvation is from the Jews."[33] Their conversation is anything but smooth, containing hints of sarcasm, sharp disagreement, and bouts of controversy, but Jesus presses on nonetheless. As their conversation comes to an end, Jesus reveals to her that he is the long-awaited and highly anticipated Messiah. In her excitement, the woman leaves her water jar by the well and hurries back into town to tell others about Jesus. Hirsch and Ford summarize, "As Jesus's ambassadors, seeking to have a *right here, right now* impact, it is imperative that we cultivate in ourselves the Jesus habit of moving past prejudiced assessments of others that we get via these initial impressions. We should work to develop a hearing ear and a seeing eye to what the Lord is saying to us about another individual."[34]

---

[32] John 4:17b-18

[33] John 4:22

[34] Alan Hirsch and Lance Ford, *Right Here, Right Now*, (Grand Rapids, MI: Baker Books, 2011), 86.

A BAPTIST WALKS INTO A BAR

Since moving back to my hometown, I have been routinely going to an Irish pub in the midtown area. It's exactly what you would imagine an Irish pub looking like and feeling like: Memorabilia lines the walls. The tables are nothing flashy, and many of them could use some carpentry work. The lighting is relatively low. The vibe is relaxed and unhurried. The people are welcoming. Who wouldn't want to hang out at a place like that?

I have made it a point to contribute to their monthly bluegrass jam by bringing my guitar and picking some tunes with the local musicians. I never miss one of these jam sessions, except in the rarest of circumstances, and I genuinely look forward to not only playing music (one of my passions) but also connecting with some of my good friends. It's become a regular thing for our little community of musicians, and those at the pub seem to look forward to us being there.

On one occasion, as the jam was winding down, I wandered over to a table with a few of my buddies. They were talking politics and religion (the two things you are never supposed to talk about). I simply sat down and began listening. Before long, a few other musicians joined us at the table, and the conversation began shifting entirely toward spiritual matters and specifically Christianity (my friends all know that I'm a pastor).

One of my buddies, who is Jewish, spoke up, "I have recently started believing in God again. Things just make more sense if he is real." Another person shared, "I am really skeptical about the whole thing. Isn't Christianity a personal journey of self-discovery? I think I can do that on my own." Round the table it went. Someone else said, "I am really an agnostic. It's great that you believe what you believe, but there is no way of really knowing if God exists." I couldn't believe what I was witnessing—people opening up about their deeply held convictions about God and faith. By this point, it was getting late. I sent my wife a text letting her know that I was going to be later than usual and not to stay up. Just then, a woman approached our table. She came right up to us and said, "Hi! I'm a lesbian, and I have been listening to your conversation. Can I join you?"

As we continued talking, many of my friends expressed their disdain for how people who claim to be Christian treat and speak to those with whom they disagree. Eyes kept glancing over in my direction. Someone finally asked, "Justin, what are your thoughts?" I wish I could say that I had been preparing a good rebuttal while listening, but I was a little caught off guard. So, I did the only thing I knew: I told them a story about Jesus.

I shared a story about Jesus from John chapter 8, where a group of religious elites catch a woman in the act of adultery and bring her to Jesus. Seeking to put Jesus to the test, they say, "Now in the Law, Moses commanded us to stone such women. So what do you say?"[35] You may know the rest of the story. Jesus then bends down and begins to write on the ground. He stands up and says to them, "Let him who is without sin among you be the first to throw a stone at her."[36] They begin dropping their stones

---

[35] John 8:5

[36] John 8:7b

as they leave, and then only Jesus and the woman are left there together. (At this point in the story, I remember looking up and everyone was leaning forward, waiting to hear how Jesus would respond to her.) He finally says to the woman, "Has no one condemned you? . . . Neither do I condemn you; go, and from now on sin no more."[37]

I remember it got quiet around the table, and then someone broke the silence and began talking again. We continued our conversation until things slowed down, and, one by one, we started packing up. As I left, I remember thinking about my earlier years of ministry. I don't know if I would have ever ventured into this setting. (What would my Christian friends think? Would this raise too many eyebrows?) But if Jesus has called his church to live S.E.N.T. lives—to live as everyday missionaries in every area of life—then it will require crossing several uncomfortable categories.

How often do we let the categories of place, people, and persuasion keep us from seeing others the way Jesus sees them? It is so much safer to avoid "that part of town." It is so much more comfortable to hang out with people "like us." It is so much easier to talk with those who share our worldview, our values, and our political views. But is that what Jesus has sent us to do? Has Jesus sent us into the world to be people who always choose what is safe, comfortable, and easy? If Jesus really has called his church to live S.E.N.T., then his church is also expected to do the hard

---

[37] John 8:10-11

missionary work of crossing categories so that we can truly see the individual.

Categories Jesus Crossed:

1. Place: Areas, regions, or spaces intentionally avoided or overlooked because of their history, reputation, or surroundings.

2. People: Persons intentionally avoided or overlooked because of their ethnicity, age, gender, socioeconomic status, lifestyle, or interests.

3. Persuasion: Subject matter intentionally avoided or overlooked because of the potential for conflict, tension, or misunderstanding.

OPPORTUNITIES, NOT INTERRUPTIONS

In the 1970s, two psychologists at Princeton University studied the effects of several situational variables on a person's willingness to help others in an emergency situation. In their classic study titled "From Jerusalem to Jericho," John Darley and Daniel Batson used the Parable of the Good Samaritan (Luke 10:25-42) as a model for designing their study. Here is the parable:

There was once a man traveling from Jerusalem to Jericho. On the way he was attacked by robbers. They took his clothes, beat him up, and went off leaving him half-dead. Luckily, a priest was on his way down the same road, but when he saw him he angled across to the other side. Then a Levite religious man showed up; he also avoided the injured man.

A Samaritan traveling the road came on him. When he saw the man's condition, his heart went out to him. He gave him first aid, disinfecting and bandaging his wounds. Then he lifted him onto his donkey, led him to an inn, and made him comfortable. In the morning he took out two silver coins and gave them to the innkeeper, saying, "Take good care of him. If it costs any more, put it on my bill— I'll pay you on my way back." (Luke 10:30-35, MSG)

The researchers gathered forty Princeton seminary students to participate in the study. They were asked to give a short presentation on one of two topics: alternative job opportunities for trained clergy or the Parable of the Good Samaritan. Once they were given their prompt, students were then told that their presentation would occur in a separate building and were subsequently told one of three things: they were already late for their presentation, they were expected immediately for their presentation, or they had a few minutes before their presentation started. All the participants began walking to the proper building and passed through an alley that contained a staged victim slumped over in the doorway. As the participants passed by, the victim coughed twice, and the researchers recorded their interactions and helping behavior.[38]

What do you think happened? Did the seminary students rise to the occasion and sacrificially help their neighbor? Did those who were preparing to give a talk on the Parable of the Good Samaritan display more situational awareness and compassion toward those around them? Did the participants' sense of hurry have any impact on their willingness to help and recognize those in need of medical attention? Darley and Batson summed up two large findings: "Subjects in a hurry were likely to offer less help than were subjects not in a hurry. Whether the subject was going to give a speech on the Parable of the Good Samaritan or not did not significantly affect his behavior on this analysis."[39] It would seem that the irony of the Parable of the Good Samaritan was being played out all over again. The most likely of candidates to offer help failed to do so (Jewish priests and Levites in the parable, and seminary students giving a presentation on the parable in the study). Darley and Batson even state in the study's conclusion, "Indeed, on several occasions, a seminary student going to give his talk on the Parable of the Good Samaritan literally stepped over the victim as he hurried on his way!" It would seem that one's sense of hurriedness presents a real barrier to seeing

---

[38] John M. Darley and Daniel Batson, "From Jericho to Jerusalem: A Study of Situational and Dispositional Variables in Helping Behavior," *Journal of Personality and Social Psychology*, no. 1 (1973): 100-108, accessed November 11, 2020, https://tinyurl.com/4m55exhw.

[39] Darley and Batson, 104.

people as Jesus did. As students frantically rushed to complete their assigned task, they inadvertently skipped over the most pressing needs around them. Their desire to meet a deadline, get to a destination, or fulfill their duty essentially blinded them to the opportunities right under their noses.

In his book titled *The Top Ten Mistakes Leaders Make*, Hans Finzel spells out one of the biggest challenges leaders face: paperwork versus "peoplework."[40] There is no question that the business world is predisposed to value paperwork over peoplework, and often the pressure to perform, complete a task, and achieve results can negatively influence how we interact with those around us. Finzel gives a simple tool for determining how we see people. He writes:

> I have devised a simple test to discover whether a person is task oriented or people oriented. It's unscientific, but completely reliable. When someone walks into your office, or wherever you happen to work, and interrupts your task at hand for the sake of conversation, how do you react? Do you view that person as an interruption or an opportunity?[41]

Do you squirm when someone disturbs your workflow? Do you become easily agitated when the conversation goes longer than expected? Does your body language communicate

---

[40] Hans Finzel, *The Top Ten Mistakes Leaders Make*, (Colorado Springs, CO: David Cook, 2007), 49.

[41] Finzel, 45.

preoccupation or attentive listening? Even if we believe that people are more important than to-do lists and tasks, often our default reactions demonstrate how we truly feel about people and what we truly value. How can we move toward seeing people as opportunities instead of interruptions?

TWO DAUGHTERS

I am always amazed at the amount of time Jesus takes to heal people through physical touch. Even though he is capable of performing instantaneous healings by simply speaking (Matt. 8:5-13; 12:9-14), he often chooses to take the time to travel to a home, touch the sick and hurting, and tarry in the company of the marginalized.

On one occasion, Jesus returns from the region of Decapolis and is greeted by a massive crowd. A man named Jairus falls at Jesus's feet and explains that his daughter, his only daughter, is dying. Jairus was a local synagogue ruler and a prominent leader within the Jewish community. Jesus immediately sets out toward Jairus's house as the large crowd presses in on him. While on the way, an anonymous woman pushes through the crowd, attempting to touch the edge of Jesus's clothing, believing that even the briefest moment of contact with him could heal her of her bleeding. The first woman in this story (Jairus's daughter) is likely well known in the community, while the other is anonymous. The first woman is experiencing a life-threatening situation, while the other's is a non-emergency. Jesus had set out on a task to heal the first woman but was interrupted by the second. How would he respond to these polar opposite requests?

The woman in the crowd makes contact with Jesus, and when he senses that power has left his body, he completely stops. You can almost sense Jairus's anticipation: "Come on! We've got to go! My daughter is hanging on by a thread! Every second counts here!" Jesus completely stops and demands to know who touched him. With so many people and so much noise, how could they possibly know? His disciple, Peter, says almost sarcastically, "Master, the people are crowding and pressing against you."[42] Jesus insists on knowing who it was. Finally, the woman comes forward and confesses. But rather than scold her or chastise her for being an interruption, Jesus says, "Daughter, your faith has healed you. Go in peace."[43]

Then, the unthinkable happens. In the blink of an eye, Jesus gains a daughter in faith but Jairus loses his. One of Jairus's servants runs over and says, "Your daughter is dead. Don't bother the teacher [Jesus] anymore."[44] Now, the story doesn't say how close they were to Jairus's house, or how long the exchange between Jesus and the woman in the crowd took, but you have to wonder, had Jesus not been interrupted, would they have made it in time to save his daughter?

Jesus responds to the news by saying, "Do not fear; only believe, and she will be well." They come to the house, and

---

[42] Luke 8:45, NIV

[43] Luke 8:48, NIV

[44] Luke 8:49, NIV

everyone is weeping and mourning over the loss of Jairus's daughter. Jesus takes Peter, James, John, and the parents into the house and takes the girl by the hand saying, "Child, arise."[45] The girl's spirit returns. She is alive again!

As a bystander in this story, I'm sure it would have been tempting to view the woman's interruption as a distraction from the task at hand. But Jesus sees everyone, from the daughter of a prominent local leader to the anonymous woman in the crowd, as worthy of his time and respect. Since Proverbs 16:9 reminds us, "The heart of a man plans his way, but the Lord establishes his steps," maybe we should learn how to view all our interactions with others as divine opportunities instead of interruptions.

I SEE YOU

For many people, meeting and making new friends can be a challenge. On top of our general reticence for stepping outside of our comfort zones in this area, a large number of people simply don't interact with very many people on a weekly basis. That could be due to personal choices, where your physical home is located, the job you have (or don't have), your stage of life—any number of circumstances. But whatever the frequency of our interactions with others, we need to be making the most of every opportunity. It almost seems silly to be sharing these simple, practical ways to "See Others like Jesus," but you would be surprised how often we need to be reminded of them. In my day-to-day routines, I can

---

[45] Luke 8:50, 54

sometimes forget to do these. However, when I do remember, I
have seen these practices drastically change the way I interact
with others—leading to new relationships, meaningful conversations, and opportunities to learn from and listen to others.

A fascinating social experiment was done in 2015 by The
Liberators on how making intentional eye contact can change
our interactions with others.[46] The experiment asked participants to willingly sit down across from a complete stranger in a
public space and maintain eye contact with them for one unin-
terrupted minute. Sounds simple enough. The results were stun-
ning. Initially, nothing special happens. It just seems as though
two complete strangers are engaging in some sort of awkward ritual. But then a few more seconds passes and something begins to
change. One of the participants can't help but crack a smile, leading to an almost avalanche effect of laughter. Others, eyes welling
up with tears, fight back their emotions until they can't take it any
longer. As the video reel continues, the full spectrum of human
emotions is displayed, and at the conclusion of the minute most
participants are seen shaking the hands of the stranger and some
even embracing with a hug. One of their videos ends with a quote
that's attributed to an American philosopher named William
James: "We are like islands in the sea, separate on the surface
but connected in the deep."[47] One minute of eye contact made all

---

[46] To learn more about the "Eye Contact Experiment" go to: www.thelibera-
tors.org/eye-contact-experiment.

[47] Probably a "misquote" found here on Wiki: www.en.wikiquote.org/wiki/
William_James

the difference in these participants' sense of connectedness with complete strangers. Can we offer a similar level of intentionality by seeing others like Jesus did?

You and I have both experienced it: Someone diverts their eyes as you pass by them on a sidewalk. Someone quickly looks in the other direction after noticing you. Someone doesn't bother to look up from their phone or computer when you ask them a question. We know how it feels to not be noticed, for our very presence to not even be acknowledged. Yet, on the flip side, most of us also know how it feels when someone treats us as though we are the most important person in the world, when someone makes eye contact with us and takes a noticeable interest in who we are and what we have to say. Making eye contact with others is the first step to seeing people like Jesus does, and it makes all the difference in the world.

YOU ARE SITTING IN MY SEAT

About a year or two ago, I walked into a local coffee shop to work on an assignment for class. I noticed that one of the seats at the bar was open and near an electrical outlet, so I quickly made myself at home and got to work. A few minutes later, the atmosphere changed in the coffee shop. A gentleman the baristas knew by name walked in, and they began talking, laughing, and preparing his drink before he even made it to the counter. After the gentleman received his drink order, he sat down right next to me and asked, "Whatcha workin' on?" I took my earbuds out and told him I was in seminary and was working on a theology paper. "Fascinating!" he said, and we began to have a great conversation about the books I had been reading and what I hoped to do professionally after I graduated. We made small talk for a few more minutes, and as our conversation came to a close he said something I will never forget: "By the way, you are sitting in my seat." "Excuse me?" I responded. "Yes," he said. "You are sitting in my seat." And he pointed to the edge of the countertop directly in front of me. After searching for a few seconds, I saw it. Sure enough, there was a small, gold plaque (the kind you would find on a trophy) fixed to the edge of the countertop, and it read "This seat belongs to Don."

Don was what you would call a "regular" at this coffee shop. He came in every day, ordered the same drink, and sat in the same seat. The baristas knew him by name, and you could tell that they all had great relationships with one another. Don's entrance into the coffee shop resembled that of Norm Peterson walking into his regular haunt in downtown Boston in the 1970s sitcom *Cheers*. "Afternoon, everybody," Norm would say, to which the *entire* bar would heartwarmingly respond, "Norm!" In the same way, Don had become someone this coffee shop looked forward to seeing and *expected* to see on a regular basis.

Don was frequenting what sociologist Ray Oldenberg refers to as a "third place." Third places are public areas used for informally gathering, hanging out, or catching up with others. Oldenberg calls where we live our "first place," where we work our "second place," and where we hang out our "third place." In their book, *Next Door as It Is in Heaven*, Brad Brisco and

Lance Ford elaborate on what a "third place" actually is: "In the most basic sense, a third place is a public setting that hosts regular, voluntary, and informal gatherings of people. It is a place to relax, a place where people enjoy visiting. Third places provide the opportunity to know and be known." [48] While most of us excel at frequenting our first and second places, it will take some intentionality to begin frequenting a third place. However, doing so will open up opportunities to "see people like Jesus" like never before. You may be surprised at who you meet, the relationships you develop, and what God has already been doing in those places.

YOU REMIND ME OF JESUS

In 2016, I attended a conference in Washington, D.C., called Praxis. It was there that I heard one of the most profound ways to compliment someone. In one of the breakout sessions, a man named Paul Sparks gave a talk about making disciples within your own neighborhood. During the talk, he mentioned a story that has always stuck with me. He said that he often tries to discover and comment on the way other people "remind him of Jesus." He will tell people, "You remind me of Jesus when you [fill in the blank]" or "You remind me of Jesus by the way you [fill in the blank]." He says that he looks for this in Christians and not-yet-Christians alike, believing that their good deeds are reflections

---

[48] Brad Brisco and Lance Ford, *Next Door as It Is in Heaven: Living Out God's Kingdom in Your Neighborhood*, (Colorado Springs, CO: NavPress, 2016), 126.

of their having been made in the image of God. By compliment-
ing people in this way, Sparks is not only establishing a relational
connection between himself and the individual but also building
bridges between those people and the Lord Jesus. A sincere and
genuine compliment is a tangible way to see others like Jesus.

A word of caution: don't try to force this into every single
interaction you have throughout your day. If you do, you may
come across as insincere or, even worse, a total creep. The most
important thing is to listen to the Holy Spirit's guidance in these
things. If the Spirit prompts you to meet someone, then do it!
If he prompts you to compliment someone you meet, then do
it! But don't force these things just so you can say that you did
them or to check them off some list. These are simply avenues for
relational connection that much of society has lost. The majority
of people do not make eye contact. The majority of people do not
take the time to learn, let alone use, your name. The majority of
people do not compliment one another. As followers of Christ, we
should strive to make relational connections with those people
God puts into our path and truly see the inherent value of those
around us. Whether we are introverted or extroverted, it's part of
our calling to see people like Jesus and to affirm the dignity of all
persons, not because of what they do or don't do but because of
who they are—image bearers of God. May God give us eyes to see
the wonder of each person he puts in our path.

QUESTIONS TO CONSIDER

1. Which category presents the largest barrier to you in being able to see people like Jesus: place, people, or persuasion? What steps can you take to change that?

2. Quickly take Hans Finzel's "peoplework versus paperwork" test on page 68 of this book. What is your default reaction? What can you do to begin viewing others more as opportunities than interruptions?

3. Try to memorize the three practical ways to see people like Jesus: make eye contact, become a regular at a "third place," and tell others how they remind you of Jesus. This week keep a journal of how doing these things changes you and your interactions with others.

Chapter 5

EAT WITH PEOPLE LIKE JESUS

"The Son of Man has come eating and drinking. . ."

Jesus

The Bible opens with a picnic, ends with a feast, and is full of
meals in between. Food is instrumental in telling God's redemptive story, with many of the major turning points revolving
around food and drink. Consider this: the first sinful act found
in the Bible is actually an act of eating. Adam and Eve disobey
God by eating from the Tree of the Knowledge of Good and
Evil: "So when the woman saw that the tree was good for food,
and that it was a delight to the eyes, and that the tree was to be
desired to make one wise, she took of its fruit and ate, and she
also gave some to her husband who was with her, and he ate."[49]
The Jewish Passover, which commemorates Israel's exodus from
Egypt, is centered on and celebrated with a full meal (Exodus
12:1-11). The giving of the Mosaic Law was confirmed with the
sharing of a meal between God and some of Israel's key leaders
on Mount Sinai. "Then Moses and Aaron, Nadab, and Abihu,

---

[49] Genesis 3:6

and seventy of the elders of Israel went up, and they saw the God of Israel. There was under his feet as it were a pavement of sapphire stone, like the very heaven for clearness. And he did not lay his hand on the chief men of the people of Israel; they beheld God, and ate and drank."[50]

The Law itself contains various guidelines for holding numerous celebrations that involve the abundance of food and drink. In Deuteronomy 14, God even requires a tithe to cover the cost of these parties!

> You shall tithe all the yield of your seed that comes from the field year by year. And before the LORD your God, in the place that he will choose, to make his name dwell there, you shall eat the tithe of your grain, of your wine, and of your oil, and the first-born of your herd and flock, that you may learn to fear the LORD your God always. And if the way is too long for you, so that you are not able to carry the tithe, when the LORD your God blesses you, because the place is too far from you, which the LORD your God chooses, to set his name there, then you shall turn it into money and bind up the money in your hand and go to the place that the LORD your God chooses and spend the money for whatever you desire—oxen or sheep or wine or strong drink, whatever your appetite craves. And

---

[50] Exodus 24:9-11

you shall eat there before the LORD your God and rejoice, you and your household."[51]

Inside the tabernacle, the place where God dwelled among the Israelites while in the wilderness, was a beautiful table arrangement. This table, complete with candles, plates, bowls, jars, jugs, and freshly baked bread, signified God's very presence among the people of Israel (Exodus 25). Richard Averbeck writes, "The combination of the daily lighting of the lampstand and associated burning of incense . . . plus the bread constantly on the table impresses one that the Lord had truly taken up residence in the tabernacle. If there is a lamp burning, incense burning and bread on the table, then someone is home."[52] As the Israelites were being led by God through the wilderness, his daily provision was seen in providing manna (bread) from heaven and water from the rock at Horeb (Exodus 16 and 17). Their destination, the Promised Land, is even described in terms of food: "a land flowing with milk and honey."[53]

These instances only scratch the surface on the number of times that food appears within the Bible's redemptive story. In fact, food and drink are so key to God's story that you could

---

[51] Deuteronomy 14:22-26

[52] Richard Averbeck, "The Holy Spirit in the Hebrew Bible and Its Connections to the New Testament," *Who's Afraid of the Holy Spirit? An Investigation into the Ministry of the Spirit of God Today,* ed. M. James Sawyer and Daniel B. Wallace, (Dallas: Biblical Studies Press, 2005), 31.

[53] Exodus 3:17

even summarize the entire Bible through them. Consider this brief summary:

- Creation: God gifts Adam and Eve with every plant yielding seed and fruit-bearing tree. He says, "You shall have them for food."[54]

- Fall: Adam and Eve eat from the forbidden tree, the Tree of the Knowledge of Good and Evil.

- Redemption: Jesus is "the bread of life" and "living water" and says, "Whoever feeds on my flesh and drinks my blood has eternal life."[55]

- Restoration: The book of Revelation details what the kingdom of God will look like at the end of all things. It's a gigantic wedding feast—the Marriage Supper of the Lamb (Revelation 19).

With food and drink being so prevalent throughout the Scriptures, it should come as no surprise that a large majority of Jesus's ministry revolved around them as well.

A PARTY ANIMAL?

Time for a pop quiz. How would you finish this statement: "The Son of Man came . . ."? Stop reading just for a second and try to complete that statement. (Don't cheat by looking below! I'll give

[54] Genesis 1:29b

[55] John 6:54a

you a hint: there are three possible answers from the Scriptures).
I have borrowed this simple quiz from Tim Chester's *A Meal with
Jesus* and have observed that the results are almost always the
same every time I give this quiz. The first answer people give is
almost always a variation of Luke 19:10 where Jesus states, "For
the Son of Man came to seek and to save the lost." On far fewer
occasions do people get the second instance where Jesus says of
himself, "For even the Son of Man came not to be served but
to serve, and to give his life as a ransom for many."[56] However,
almost no one gets the third instance. The third instance is this:
"The Son of Man came eating and drinking."[57] Here is the passage:

> For John the Baptist has come eating no bread and
> drinking no wine, and you say, "He has a demon."
> The Son of Man has come eating and drinking, and
> you say, "Look at him! A glutton and a drunkard, a
> friend of tax collectors and sinners!" Yet wisdom is
> justified by all her children.[58]

Tim Chester does a great job explaining why this is so significant: "The first two are statements of purpose. *Why* did Jesus
come? He came to serve, to give his life as a ransom, to seek and
save the lost. The third is a statement of method. *How* did Jesus

---

[56] Mark 10:45

[57] Matthew 11:19 and Luke 7:34

[58] Luke 7:33-35

come? He came eating and drinking."[59] In other words, sharing meals with others was central to Jesus's ministry strategy, and the common table was one of his greatest ministry tools. How about you? How about the local church? Do we do the same? Brisco and Ford write:

> The Gospel accounts corroborate what Jesus had to say about his method of operation. Eating and drinking with others is a constant theme throughout the biblical history of how and what Jesus did during his earthly ministry. Churches are most often found meeting. Jesus was most often found eating. If you were to bump into him on the streets of Jerusalem, he would have been more likely to invite you to a barbecue than to a Bible study.[60]

Maybe you've never noticed it before, but Jesus is always eating and drinking with others through the Gospels. Many of the verses we highlight in the Gospels are words Jesus spoke within the context of a shared meal. Here are a few examples:

- "I came not to call the righteous, but sinners." Jesus spoke these words in Matthew 9:13 while he

---

[59] Tim Chester, *A Meal with Jesus: Discovering Grace, Community, and Mission Around the Table*, (Wheaton, IL: Crossway, 2011), 12.

[60] Brad Brisco and Lance Ford, *Next Door as It Is in Heaven: Living Out God's Kingdom in Your Neighborhood*, (Colorado Springs, CO: NavPress, 2016), 110.

was sitting around a table with tax collectors and sinners.

- "There is nothing outside a person that by going into him can defile him, but the things that come out of a person are what defile him." Jesus spoke these words in Mark 7:15 while sharing a meal with a group of Pharisees and scribes.

- "For the Son of Man came to seek and to save the lost." Jesus said these words in Luke 19:10 while sharing a meal at a chief tax collector's house.

- "By this all people will know that you are my disciples, if you have love for one another." Jesus spoke these words in John 13:35 while he was with his disciples eating the Last Supper.

- For even more examples, refer to Appendix C: More Meals of Jesus.

Thus, is it fair to think of Jesus as a party animal? While he certainly ate and drank frequently throughout his ministry, sharing meals with others was not an end in and of itself. Jesus leveraged the meal for the mission on which he was sent, calling people to him and challenging them to follow him with their whole lives. We, too, can leverage the shared meal for mission, creating opportunities to develop deeper relationships with others and invite them to follow Christ.

RADICALLY INCLUSIVE

Think back with me to your high school days and eating lunch in the cafeteria. When I was in high school, the upperclassmen were allowed to go off campus for lunch, leaving only the freshmen and sophomores in the cafeteria. Every day, my friends and I would enter through the double doors and take our places at the table, sitting in the same spot and eating with the same people. A quick glance around the room revealed the same about everyone else. Everyone had their own group to which they belonged: athletes, brainiacs, nerds, band geeks, and on and on it went. Back then, one thing was for sure, I wouldn't be caught dead trying to sit in a different spot or with another group of people. It would have been social suicide! Meals, even as early as high school, were societal separators. They drew crystal clear lines around those with whom we were allowed to associate and those with whom we were not. And it was the same, if not more so, in Jesus's day.

In Luke 5 we read:

> After this he went out and saw a tax collector named Levi, sitting at the tax booth. And he said to him, "Follow me." And leaving everything, he rose and followed him. And Levi made him a great feast in his house, and there was a large company of tax collectors and others reclining at table with them. And the Pharisees and their scribes grumbled at his disciples, saying, "Why do you eat and drink with tax collectors and sinners?" And Jesus answered

them, "Those who are well have no need of a phy-
sician, but those who are sick. I have not come to
call the righteous but sinners to repentance."[61]

As a twenty-first century Westerner, it's hard to grasp why a
first-century Pharisee would make such a big deal about a party.
But please hear me on this: the real problem is not the party; it's
the guest list. Recall that during the life and ministry of Jesus,
the people of Israel were under Roman rule and longed for the
day when they would experience national renewal and restoration through God's Messiah. In the Pharisees' eyes, Rome was
the complete antithesis to the nation of Israel. While fraternizing
with the enemy was unthinkable, there was almost nothing more
traitorous than working for them as a tax collector. Tax collectors
were regarded by most as "playing for the other team" and inher-
ently corrupt. But here we have God's Messiah partying it up with
these well-known "traitors," as well as some of the local riffraff.
It's clear from the Pharisees' question that they thought Jesus was
guilty by association. How could Jesus possibly be exposed to
such impurity and immorality and come out unscathed?

On a separate occasion, Jesus is invited to eat at another
Pharisee's house. Luke 11:37-41 states:

While Jesus was speaking, a Pharisee asked him
to dine with him, so he went in and reclined at
table. The Pharisee was astonished to see that he

---

did not first wash before dinner. And the Lord said to him, "Now you Pharisees cleanse the outside of the cup and of the dish, but inside you are full of greed and wickedness. You fools! Did not he who made the outside make the inside also? But give as alms those things that are within, and behold, everything is clean for you.

In addition to excluding certain persons from their table fellowship, the Pharisees were also obsessed with a religious ritual: cleanliness. They took great care to ritually wash their hands before eating, as well as any plate, bowl, cup, or utensil that would come in contact with them during the meal. This was to ensure their personal purity. Their rituals had become their religion. So you can imagine their utter shock when the rabbi from Nazareth doesn't wash beforehand but digs right into the meal! The Pharisees probably thought, "Who knows where this guy's hands have been?" Actually, Jesus's hands have been getting quite "dirty" before this meal. Consider what, and more specifically *whom*, he has touched:

- **A leper:** "And Jesus stretched out his hand and touched him, saying, 'I will; be clean.'" (Luke 5:13)
- **The crowds/multitudes:** "And all the crowd sought to touch him, for power came out from him and healed them all." (Luke 6:19)
- **A bier on which a dead man lay:** "Then he came up and touched the bier, and the bearers stood

still. And he said, 'Young man, I say to you, arise.'"
(Luke 7:14)

- **A local prostitute:** "Now when the Pharisee who
  had invited him saw this, he said to himself, 'If this
  man were a prophet, he would have known who
  and what sort of woman this is who is touching
  him, for she is a sinner.'" (Luke 7:39)

- **A diseased woman:** "She came up behind him and
  touched the fringe of his garment, and immediately
  her discharge of blood ceased." (Luke 8:44)

- **A dead girl:** "But taking her by the hand he called,
  saying, 'Child, arise.'" (Luke 8:54)

Jesus's ambivalence toward eating with unwashed hands
did not result from a disregard for sanitation. No, it was much
deeper than that. The Pharisees had allowed their pursuit of
purity and cleanliness to produce an elitist faith that excluded
others, especially the marginalized, from participating. Chester
is helpful, saying:

> The effect of the ritual cleansing was not only to
> create boundaries with Gentiles, but also with the
> poor. The religious elite had created a system of
> moral respectability that only the wealthy could
> ever hope to maintain. Only the rich had the time
> and money to do all the required ritual cleansing.

You can't be ritually clean in a slum. This was bourgeois spirituality.[62]

Jesus's radical inclusion stemmed from his contagious holiness. He wasn't afraid of others' moral impurity rubbing off on him. His contact with others doesn't result in his defilement but in their restoration. His table fellowship with others doesn't result in a cross-contamination of immorality or wickedness. Rather, his gracious presence with the spiritually wayward and impure steadily wooed them toward the call of discipleship, toward leaving their former way of life, toward taking up their cross and following him.

A LOST ART

While my wife, Lindsey, and I were dating, she had a job working at the University of Florida's English Language Institute as a language assistant. Her job afforded her endless opportunities to not only help exchange students learn to speak English, but also to build cross-cultural bridges for Christ. Every so often, I would stop by to see Lindsey teaching her class, and she would introduce me to a few of her students. We got to know several of the students very well and, on one occasion, were invited for dinner at a student's apartment. "Dinner is at 10 p.m." (He was from Saudi Arabia, and dinner is much later in the evening for them than Americans are used to). I'm usually asleep by 10 p.m., but I

---

62 Tim Chester, *A Meal with Jesus: Discovering Grace, Community, and Mission Around the Table*, (Wheaton, IL: Crossway, 2011),, 22.

pumped myself full of caffeine so I could make it through dinner and not faceplant into my food. When the night came, we arrived a little early for dinner. Our host opened the door, welcomed us, and presented us with the biggest plate of fruit I'd seen in a long time. A mountain of strawberries and grapes, easily a foot tall, precariously sat atop a flimsy paper plate on a coffee table in the living room. I took a quick glance around his apartment. There was no dinner table in sight. "Where are we going to eat?" I wondered. "Maybe right here on the couch?"

The next thing I knew, our host asked us to help prepare the floor for dinner. Handing us a few trash bags, he instructed us to rip them apart so they would create a kind of disposable mat in the middle of the floor. He brought the main course from the oven and placed it right on top of the trash bags. Two 9x13 aluminum foil pans full of chicken, rice, and who knows what else were placed before us. It smelled amazing, and there was an abundance of food for just the three of us. As we took our places around the food, another mealtime staple was noticeably missing: utensils. We soon realized we would be eating with our hands (it's not as barbaric as it sounds). Our host showed us how to eat with our hands and not look like complete morons. We ate until we were satisfied, all the while talking about our faith and asking him questions about his. We finally said our goodbyes a little after 1 a.m. Looking back, it's one of my all-time favorite meals. Our host, who was Muslim, single, and a college-aged man living more than 7,300 miles away from his hometown, showed Lindsey and me what many successful, married, self-professed Christians struggle to show toward their own families and friends—how to fully engage in and enjoy sharing a meal.

It probably comes as no surprise, but the majority of American families share meals together less frequently than they did fifty years ago.[63] Traditionally, the evening meal represented the locus of connection and belonging for a family, a communal experience that fostered a sense of togetherness and helped strengthen the familial bond. But now, things are changing.

More and more people are choosing to eat alone and on the go. Restaurants are changing their seating layouts, and producers of frozen dinners are changing their packaging to cater to this new social reality. Tables specifically set up for one guest and smaller, more portable packaging are just some of the ways these major industries are adapting to these new preferences. Even among multi-person households, nearly half of all meals are consumed alone.[64] If households are intentional enough to share a meal together, mealtimes are, on average, drastically shorter than they used to be.

It's not uncommon to attend a dinner in someone's house only to hear the constant drone of the television in the background. Meals are being consumed among technological distractions, making us less present with the people sitting next to us

---

[63] Robert Putnam, *Bowling Alone: The Collapse and Revival of American Community*, (New York, NY: Simon and Schuster, 2000), 100.

[64] Shelley Balanko, "Food and Beverage Analytics: Hartman Eating Occasions Compass," Hartman Group, last modified 2017, accessed May 2020, https://tinyurl.com/22mze543

and talking with us. Kitchen tables at home, conference tables at work, and coffee tables in local shops now all have one thing in common: cellphones. A quick glance at the tops of any of these tables will almost always reveal a cellphone, or multiple cellphones, placed between people sharing a meal, conducting business, or simply catching up. As eating with others becomes more of a lost art, we will become increasingly disconnected, relating to one another in distanced and superficial ways. Yet the world is longing for people to eat with them like Jesus.

INTEGRATION OVER ADDITION

A few years ago, Lindsey and I were invited by a group of friends to take a weekend camping trip in Myrtle Beach, South Carolina. One evening after dinner, the guys decided to set up some hammocks in the trees around our campsite. While relaxing, we began talking about our small group and some new ideas we would like to incorporate into our weekly gatherings. Tom suggested we immediately begin including a meal during our small group gathering. As the host and leader of the group, Tom wanted to gauge our interest in sharing a meal with the other members on a regular basis. After a few seconds of silence, Brett chimed in, "That's a cool idea, but I don't think it's going to work. I think it's just too expensive."

"Really?" I said. "It's not *that* expensive."

Tom then asked, "Brett, do you plan on eating every night?"

"Well, yeah . . . of course," he said.

"Then just bring that," Tom said. "Just bring what you were planning to eat, and come ready to share it with others." I was struck by the simplicity of Tom's statement: *Just bring what you were planning to eat, and come ready to share it with others.* Brett was operating out of an addition mindset, while Tom was operating out of an integration mindset.

The thought of sharing a meal with three people this week (one of whom is not a member of your local church) might sound daunting if you are thinking about it in terms of "addition." With addition, we envision piling more things on top of our already busy schedules and trying to cram more meetings and appointments into our daily routines. That type of thinking is not sustainable over the long run and will lead even the most time-efficient, productive people into burnout. Instead, work toward adopting an "integration" mindset. Take your normal, everyday routine of eating and infuse it with gospel intentionality.

"I'm too busy. How will I add this to my schedule?" some may ask. Don't think about adding a meal to your schedule. Rather, pick a meal you plan to eat and invite someone to join you. Most people already eat three times a day, seven days a week. That's a total of twenty-one meals a week. Let's pick three of those meals and use that time to build deeper relationships with others. Some may wonder, "It's too expensive. How will I afford this?" Most people have plenty of food to share with others, so begin with what you have. It's better to share a simple meal than to forgo an opportunity because you can't serve an extravagant one. Remember, the goal is not to impress but to connect.

BE ALL THERE

During holiday meals, I remember always wanting to sit at the "grown-ups' table." Don't get me wrong, being the youngest in my family certainly had its perks, but the evening meal was not one of them. I, along with my sister, cousins, and whoever else happened to be there, were stuck in mealtime purgatory, bound in eternal chains at the "kids' table." I'm being a little dramatic, but our table just didn't have the same vibe as the adults'. Laughter, stories, and a sense of belonging and acceptance oozed from the grown-ups' table in a way that was simply contagious. I wanted to be there. Heck, everyone wanted to be there. That's what it must've been like to share a meal with Jesus.

I've had thousands of meals since then. Some of those meals were life-changing experiences with friends or family, while others were seemingly insignificant. However, the meals in which I have seen God work in other people's lives all have three common elements of table fellowship. These suggestions are simple but, when intentionally put into practice, open up a space for relationships to deepen and to join God in his mission.

Imagine for a moment that you sit down to a meal with a new friend. You don't know them very well, but there is something about this person that intrigues you and you'd like to get to know them better. As you sit down to the meal, you realize that your new friend is entirely focused on you. Their eyes are not wandering around the room, but instead they are concentrating on you. They lean forward to hear what you are saying as you speak, their body language communicates that they are genuinely interested in what you have to say. When they ask you a question, they actually listen to your response. They ask questions about you, your upbringing, your family, your hobbies—piecing together your life and making you feel like the most important person in the room. They never check their watch, and they seem like they could sit with you all day. The ding of a cellphone notification is never heard (at least not from the phone of your new friend), and they are not distracted by the other people in the room or the tasks that await them later in the day. They are just there, *with you*. Would you say that sounds like a good lunch? You'd probably want to hang out with this new friend again.

Jim Elliot famously stated, "Wherever you are, be all there."[65] In other words, wherever you find yourself, give that place, those people, and that purpose your undivided attention and your absolute focus. When you do this, you are being present to those around you, and it will be noticeable. Being present also communicates that you really care for and are invested in getting to know those with whom you are sharing a meal.

A simple way to start becoming more present is this: try having only one conversation at your next meal. Don't start a side conversation with the person sitting next to you or quickly respond to a text message from someone who isn't even at the table. Having one conversation doesn't mean one person will do all of the talking. It simply means that you are actively listening

---

[65] Jim Elliot, *The Journals of Jim Elliot*, ed. Elizabeth Elliot, (Grand Rapids, MI: Revell, 1978), 278.

and genuinely engaging with the people at the table. When you do this, you will be "all there."

ASKING GOOD QUESTIONS

Just as our guests were walking out the front door, they turned and said, "Thanks again for having us over. We had a great time."

"We did, as well. Let's do it again soon," we responded. We closed the door and began what Lindsey likes to call "the dinner debrief." This usually takes place as we clear the dishes from the table and begin cleaning the kitchen. As we played back the evening in our minds, we realized that we now knew a lot more about our new friends—where they were from, where they now worked, their church background, a little bit about their families, what they did for fun, and so on. As we continued to rewind our conversation, we came to the stark conclusion that even though we knew a lot about them, they didn't know diddly-squat about us. We had been keeping the conversation going all night by simply asking questions and letting our new friends tell their story. Once they would stop talking, we'd ask another question. We were not firing off a battery of interrogative requests, we were just being inquisitive.

We then realized that our new friends had never *once* asked us a question. They had ample opportunity to do so but simply never did. After all, we were not doing the talking, they were. We weren't upset. We actually thought it was kind of funny. Our guests had had a great time and wanted to spend more time with us the following week, but knew almost nothing about us. Maybe you have had a similar experience with others, but Lindsey and I have seen this reality play out over and over again. People like to talk about themselves, and when you ask good questions, not only do people feel the freedom to share about their lives but you also begin to understand more about their hearts.

There is a difference between a question that invites story-telling and one that invites a quick response. Some people like to think about the difference between these two as open-ended versus closed-ended questions. For example, "Do you work at a car dealership?" is a closed-ended question, whereas "How did you start working at a car dealership?" is more open-ended. And while these are good distinctions to make, I think it's more help-ful to think of conversations in terms of storytelling versus short answers. Short-answer questions do not usually move the con-versation forward, and they very rarely reveal another person's opinions, feelings, or dreams. Storytelling conversations, how-ever, invite others to share something about their lives and, in so doing, open up a bit more about who they really are.

Here are a few great "lead-ins" that invite storytelling:

- Tell me about a time when you . . .
- Tell me the story of how God led you to . . .
- What were the conversations you had that led you . . .
- What was the pivotal moment for you in . . .
- Tell me about the day you realized that God had . . .
- What were the steps that got you from . . .

- What are some things you've learned from . . .
- How do you think your experiences in _____ have influenced . . .

Notice that not all of these lead-ins are actually questions. Some of them are requests, asking others to provide you with a literal story from their lives (that's why I think "storytelling" is a better distinction than "open-ended"). I have found that, more often than not, the answers to these questions get a great conversation started. And when we are present with others and listen to the Spirit of God, we will know what to ask next.

NAPKIN IN YOUR LAP AND PHONES OFF THE TABLE

While not all technology is necessarily bad, limiting technology can be beneficial when eating with people like Jesus. Putting on some soft background music during a meal or a hangout can contribute to the overall comfort of the experience, but you can easily overdo it. Performing a quick "technology audit" of your home before having folks over can be a fun and revealing exercise. In *Bowling Alone*, Robert Putnam highlights the prevalence television has in the American household. He writes, "Roughly half of all Americans—married and single, parents and childless—report watching television while eating dinner, and nearly one-third do so during breakfast and lunch. By the end of the twentieth century television had become omnipresent in

Americans' lives."[66] Keeping the ball game on TV or tuning into the evening news during a meal will not only distract you but will also send the wrong message to your family, friends, and guests.

The only piece of technology more prevalent at the dinner table than the television is the smartphone. I like asking the question posed by Simon Sinek:

> What if I were to hold my phone while talking to you. I'm not checking it. It's not buzzing. It's not beeping. I'm just holding it. Do you feel, at this moment, that you are the most important thing to me right now? No, you do not. . . . When we show up to a meeting, or a lunch, or a dinner, with our colleagues, our clients, our friends, or our families, and we put the phone on the table, we have announced to everyone in the room that they are not that important to us.[67]

By putting your phones away, turning off the television, and giving others your undivided attention, you will be sending a clear message: you are important to me. By limiting technology, you will be establishing a counter-cultural meal experience that will help you eat with others just like Jesus.

---

[66] Robert Putnam, *Bowling Alone: The Collapse and Revival of American Community*, 227.

[67] Simon Sinek, https://www.youtube.com/watch?v=HTGRMWhclgM

Imagine a table fellowship characterized by grace, belonging, and hope. Imagine a table fellowship where the licentious and the liberated, the broken and the restored, the marginalized and the mainstream could experience a taste of the kingdom of God. Jesus ate and drank in such a way. Let's follow him.

QUESTIONS TO CONSIDER

1. Think back on your life. Which meals have been your favorite? Apart from the delicious food, what made them so special?

2. How do Jesus's radically inclusive eating habits challenge your life? Are there people you have intentionally or unknowingly excluded? What are you going to do about it?

3. Which of the following—being present, asking good questions, and limiting technology—do you need to work on the most? What small change can you make to help foster these habits?

Chapter 6

NEIGHBOR PEOPLE LIKE JESUS

"The Word became flesh and blood,
and moved into the neighborhood."

John 1:14, MSG

"Don't think of the doctrine of the incarnation as doctrine.
The incarnation is a story of passion."

Hugh Halter

My denominational "tribe," so to speak, is Southern Baptist, and I'll be the first to admit that we don't give much thought to the incarnation. Sure, we bring it up around the Christmas holiday each year and sing a few songs about baby Jesus asleep in a manager, but that's about as far as it goes. But more than simply being a "nice thought," the incarnation of Christ has profound implications for how the church does local ministry. Rediscovering the richness of the incarnation can unearth the motivation and methodology for loving those around us and embodying the gospel in our own neighborhoods.

The word incarnation literally means "to take on flesh," and though most of us have heard this word before, do we really understand why there even was an incarnation in the first place? In the beginning of the Gospel of John, he writes, "And the Word [Jesus] became flesh and dwelt among us." That's great, but why? In chapter two of the book of Philippians, the apostle Paul writes, "[Jesus] emptied himself, by taking the form of a servant, being born in the likeness of men. And being found in human form, he humbled himself by becoming obedient to the point of death." That's great, but why did he do that? An easy answer to these questions would be to say that "God loves us" and then move on to something else. Or, one could explain that God became human to deal with humanity's sin problem so that we could, once again, be in right relationship with him. And while that's all true, the incarnation of Christ reveals something more about God that goes far beyond a Sunday school answer or a theological equation. The incarnation reveals God's heart and should inspire us.

A BURNING, YEARNING FEELING INSIDE

I have an Apple iPhone. Every so often, my phone will alert me that it (by itself!) has arranged my pictures into a new video compilation, including themed background music and the perfect mix of favorited and funny photos. Without fail, these videos always seem to produce a couple of tears and send me longing for days gone by. Only after I've had the opportunity to privately bawl a bit do I even dare to show my wife and kids! It's amazing what a couple of family photos and some misty mood music can do to me.

There is a longing in us all to return to the good old days and to enjoy the experiences, relationships, and time that brought us so many fond memories. For some, it's the memory of a family vacation. For others, it's the memory of being with a beloved relative or friend. But whatever the case may be, there is a burning, yearning feeling inside all of us to return to that time and place and to be with those people. And it's the same for God.

Genesis 1 and 2 make it obvious that God thoroughly delighted in his creation. He makes light and calls it good. He makes land and sea and sees that it is good. He makes plants and vegetation on the earth and sees that it is good. He makes the stars, sun, and moon and sees that they are good. He makes every living creature in the waters and on earth and calls them good. Then, he makes male and female in his own image, takes a step back, beholds his creation, and declares that it is all very good. God then rests in the completion and soaks up the goodness of the work of his hands. A perfect world. Perfect companionship between God and man. The peace of God experienced in every place, relationship, and occasion. True Paradise.

And then Adam and Eve make the terrible decision to disobey God. They eat from the Tree of the Knowledge of Good and Evil. Did God know this would happen? Absolutely. But in his great love, he chose to create man and woman with the capacity to make choices. Their sin, which distorted and disrupted God's perfect design, ran havoc throughout all creation. Everything they once knew changed with that decision. And from that moment forward, God began to work out his plan of redemption in all of creation, knowing full well that one day he would send his own Son in the flesh to do for humanity what we could never even dream of doing for ourselves. God has a burning, yearning feeling that fuels his passion for what was lost.

This is the motivation for the mission. This is what drove Jesus "to take on flesh" and to step into the mess of humanity. Don't miss this: The story of the Bible reveals God's heart to restore, recover, and redeem. He desperately desires that all things be brought back to the way they were, to experience the "good old days" once again with all his creation. It's the greatest rescue mission of all time.

This is also the *why* for living missionally within our local contexts. God's passion should feed the passion of the local church and drive us to enter into the life of our neighborhood. Hugh Halter writes, "That is the *why* of incarnation, and if you don't stop to ponder why Jesus came, you will most likely miss the passion God wants to give you for living incarnationally for those around you."[68] Maybe you've lived in your neighborhood for years and have never been intentional about meeting your neighbors. Or perhaps you just moved to a new city or subdivision where the busyness of unpacking and getting settled has taken priority over meeting the folks around you. Whatever the case may be, it's never too late to start because our immediate

---

[68] Hugh Halter, *Flesh: Bringing the Incarnation Down to Earth.* (Colorado Springs, CO: David C. Cook, 2014), 31.

mission field rarely changes: it's the street on which we live. As Christ followers, we must see that God has called us to embody the gospel on the very street where we live and among the very people we call neighbors. Loving your neighbors begins with this understanding: You have been sent to live in such a way that makes the kingdom of God tangible in your neighborhood.

LOOPHOLES OF LOVE

When a sharp lawyer sought to "test" Jesus regarding the Law, he had no idea with whom he was speaking. This "expert" in the Law was actually speaking to the very Author of the Law himself. And after asking, "Teacher, what shall I do to inherit eternal life?"[69] the Author of the Law quickly throws a question back at him. Jesus responds by saying, "What is written in the Law? How do you read it?"[70] The lawyer thought for a moment and then gave a well-studied answer: "That you love the Lord your God with all your passion and prayer and muscle and intelligence—and that you love your neighbor as well as you do yourself."[71] Jesus responds, in essence, saying, "You have answered correctly; do this, and you will live."[72] With his answer, the Author of the Law struck a nerve within the heart of the "expert." The lawyer knew he was neither a perfect man, nor had he perfectly practiced what

---

[69] Luke 10:25b

[70] Luke 10:26

[71] Luke 10:27, MSG

[72] Luke 10:28

he preached. And he, just like so many who have recognized that God's moral standard is too high, began to immediately search for a loophole in the Law. Seeking to justify himself, the Scriptures say, in a last-ditch effort, he asks one final question of Jesus: "And who is my neighbor?"[73]

The lawyer sought to define the word "neighbor" in the most convenient and comfortable way possible. Perhaps if the standard for what it meant to "love your neighbor as yourself" was slightly lower, he'd still have a chance get on the good side of God and "inherit eternal life." But Jesus never lowers the standard of righteousness; he actually raises it. Here is what happened next:

> Jesus answered by telling a story. "There was once a man traveling from Jerusalem to Jericho. On the way he was attacked by robbers. They took his clothes, beat him up, and went off leaving him half-dead. Luckily, a priest was on his way down the same road, but when he saw him he angled across to the other side. Then a Levite religious man showed up; he also avoided the injured man. A Samaritan traveling the road came on him. When he saw the man's condition, his heart went out to him. He gave him first aid, disinfecting and bandaging his wounds. Then he lifted him onto his donkey, led him to an inn, and made him comfortable. In the morning he took out two silver coins and gave

---

[73] Luke 10:29b

them to the innkeeper, saying, 'Take good care of him. If it costs any more, put it on my bill—I'll pay you on my way back.'

"What do you think? Which of the three became a neighbor to the man attacked by robbers?"

"The one who treated him kindly," the religion scholar responded. Jesus said, "Go and do the same."[74]

By the end of their exchange, the lawyer's original question of "Who is my neighbor?" becomes overshadowed by the more important question posed by Jesus: "Which of the three became a neighbor?" Go back and read it again. The wounded man in the parable is not given a specific identity—not a single cultural identifier apart from where he was traveling. The fact that the wounded man is anonymous suggests that *anyone* and *everyone* is ultimately our neighbor.

There are no loopholes in the Law when it comes to loving one's neighbor. Differences based on ethnicity, socioeconomic status, sexual orientation, gender, and age become obsolete and entirely irrelevant in the call to love your neighbor as yourself. In the parable, the true neighbor was the one the lawyer would have least expected. It was neither the Jewish priest nor the Levite religious man but rather the unlikely Samaritan who was the true neighbor because he took action, stepped in, and got involved. It

---

[74] Luke 10:30-37 MSG

was his heart, and his heart alone, that went out to his neighbor in need.

The lawyer was looking for a loophole of love, an excuse for not loving others, an exemption from having to care for others as he did for himself. He had hoped that his conversation with the Author of the Law would have exposed an exemption, but he was mistaken. Jesus instead underlined and highlighted the high call to unrestricted and indiscriminate neighborly love, a love that ultimately reflects that of the Father.

WHICH GOLDEN RULE?

Toward the end of the Sermon on the Mount, Jesus fleshes out the principle inherent within the command "love your neighbor as yourself." He states, "So whatever you wish that others would do to you, do also to them, *for this is the Law and the Prophets*" (emphasis added).[75] In other words, when Jesus's followers obeyed this teaching, when they really were displaying neighborly love, they would be living out the sum total of the Old Testament Law and Prophets. And while many of us know this statement as the "Golden Rule," could it be that we are obeying a variation of this command and not Jesus's actual words? Which Golden Rule are we really following?

It may come as a surprise to some, but Jesus was not the first person to speak of the Golden Rule. Many of the major world religions and several ancient philosophers took their swing at the

---

[75] Matthew 7:12

proverbial "Golden Rule," summarizing the ethical teachings of their day in their own personal renditions. Though many versions exist, they are not all the same. We may recognize Jesus's words in our hearts but may be following another's rule in our actions.

One of the oldest variations of the Golden Rule is framed in the negative. Confucius, the ancient Chinese philosopher, summarized his Golden Rule this way: "Do not impose on others what you do not wish for yourself."[76] Zoroaster, the Persian philosopher, shared his rendition of the Golden Rule like this: "That character is best that doesn't do to another what isn't good for itself." Even the famous first-century Jewish Rabbi Hillel put his spin on it: "What is hateful to yourself, don't do to another."[77] And while these are similar to Jesus's words, they do not capture the essence of neighborly love. This is a minimalistic form of the Golden Rule because it requires minimal obligations to others: Don't think bad thoughts about them. Don't speak negatively about them. Don't cause them any harm. And while these are good parameters to practice, I would argue that if you followed this variation of the Golden Rule, you could "love your neighbor" by simply *ignoring* them.

This Golden Rule of minimums is likely what many self-professed Christians follow in everyday life. We go about our daily lives trying to be as nice as we can to as many people as we can

---

[76] Russell Freedman and Frédéric Clément, *Confucius: The Golden Rule*, (Holt McDougal, 2006), 30.

[77] Harry Gensler, *Ethics and the Golden Rule: Do Unto Others*, (Routledge, 2013), 37.

and hope that others return the favor. Many may even believe that if they mind their own business then they are off the hook! However, not hating our neighbor doesn't mean we will actively seek to love them. And Jesus is calling his church to more than passive neighboring.

Another variation on Jesus's Golden Rule is that it is love based on your choosing—you pick who to help and who to care for. In essence, you get to choose your neighbor. This was the exemption in the Law that the lawyer had hoped to discover when he asked Jesus, "And who is my neighbor?" What he really wanted to know was, "Who may I exclude? Who do I *not* have to love?" Most of us choose to love those who love us in return. We choose a love of reciprocity, a mutually beneficial love where if you "give a little" you can "get a little." Still, Jesus calls his church to more. In Luke 6:32-36, Jesus says:

> If you love those who love you, what benefit is that to you? For even sinners love those who love them. And if you do good to those who do good to you, what benefit is that to you? For even sinners do the same. And if you lend to those from whom you expect to receive, what credit is that to you? Even sinners lend to sinners, to get back the same amount. But love your enemies, and do good, and lend, expecting nothing in return, and your reward will be great, and you will be sons of the Most High, for he is kind to the ungrateful and the evil. Be merciful, even as your Father is merciful.

This is what makes Jesus's Golden Rule different from all the rest. His version is framed in the positive. Listen to his words again: "So whatever you wish that others would do to you, do also to them, for this is the Law and the Prophets." Jesus wasn't calling his followers to a minimal or reciprocal love, but to a sacrificial love. This kind of love sees a need and takes action; it willingly gets involved. The reality is we cannot ignore our neighbors, nor do we get to choose our neighbors. Our neighbors are those people God places in our path for us to sacrificially serve with no strings attached. We have been sent to display an unexpected love that expects nothing in return.

Maybe you are already doing this, but for those who aren't yet, doing so will require you to take more responsibility for those around you and to assume an increased measure of owner-ship concerning the well-being of your neighbors. The late Fred Rogers, founder of Mister Rogers' Neighborhood, said, "We live in a world in which we need to share responsibility. It's easy to say, 'It's not my child, not my community, not my world, not my problem.' Then there are those who see the need and respond. I consider those people my heroes."[78]

FROM "STRANGER-HOOD" TO NEIGHBORHOOD

What would it look like for you to literally love your actual neigh-bors? In their book *The Art of Neighboring,* Jay Pathak and Dave

---

[78] Fred Rogers (1994), quoted in Tyler Huckabee, "11 Mr. Rogers Quotes Every Christian Should Read," *Relevant Magazine*, November 22, 2019, accessed August 27, 2021, https://tinyurl.com/3vxb8mjd.

Runyon ask this very simple, yet direct question: "When Jesus was asked to reduce everything in the Bible into one command he said: Love God with everything you have *and* love your neighbor as yourself. What if he meant that we should love our actual neighbors? You know, the people who live right next door."[79] While we could get lost in how this might look different for each person, one thing is for sure: loving our actual neighbors most certainly involves opening our homes. The practice of hospitality is central to the habit of neighboring people like Jesus.

In the Bible, the Greek word for hospitality is derived from two separate Greek words: *philos*, one of the Greek words for "love," and *xenos*, meaning "a stranger or foreigner." That may not mean much to you at this moment, but for Lindsey and me, it changed everything. As I mentioned, I was raised in the South. From a very early age, I was indoctrinated in the philosophy of "Southern hospitality." I know how to be polite. I know how to entertain guests and to make small talk. I can make a pretty good pitcher of sweet tea. And I have even had Sunday dinner with "the preacher" on more than one occasion. But as Lindsey and I uncovered more about hospitality from the Scriptures, we came to a stark realization: biblical hospitality and Southern hospitality are not always one and the same. In fact, many times, they directly clash with one another.

---

[79] Dave Runyon and Jay Pathak, *The Art of Neighboring: Building Genuine Relationships Right Outside Your Door*, (Grand Rapids, MI: Baker Books, 2012), 15.

Southern hospitality does not concern itself so much with welcoming the stranger as it does with entertaining guests. Southern hospitality *takes* room while biblical hospitality *makes* room. And while Lindsey and I both knew how to entertain guests of our own choosing, we lacked experience in making an intentional effort in reaching out to those around us, to many of the people we'd still consider "strangers." Yes, we lived in a traditional neighborhood and had neighbors all around us, but we felt as though we really lived in a "stranger-hood."

From that moment forward, we made a commitment to take a "next step" with whomever God put in our path within our neighborhood. Though we didn't have a formulaic approach to this, many of our "next steps" were similar in nature: If we saw someone we didn't know, we would take the initiative to introduce ourselves and learn their names. If we ran into our neighbors outside, we would strike up a conversation and get to know them a little more, discovering something new about them. We made an effort to open our home regularly, inviting new people over for dinner. We welcomed newcomers to the neighborhood with a gift. We took food to friends going through tough seasons of life. In every instance and through every small act of hospitality, we strove to create a space of welcome where relationships could flourish and God's Spirit could work. It didn't happen overnight or without struggle, but with time our "stranger-hood" began to subtly shift.

I wish I could say that embracing this way of life was easy and always fun, but our experiment with hospitality has had its share of frustrations. It was far easier to convince ourselves that we should *not* be hospitable to our neighbors and to make any number of excuses as to why it was a good idea *not* to open our home. Yet we had an unrelenting conviction that God wanted us to use our home, one of our greatest resources, to serve others. In *The Simplest Way to Change the World*, Brandon Clements and Dustin Willis shed some light on why many of us find it difficult to open our homes to others around us. They suggest that four cultural currents are actively working against hospitable impulses.[80] Many of us "swim" in these currents, completely unaware of how they may be influencing our underlying beliefs and thoughts. The currents of isolation, relaxation, entertainment, and busyness can provide the fuel for willingly opting out of hospitality and choosing something more self-serving. After all, withdrawing into our own private retreats, binge-watching our favorite shows, and running from one activity to the next certainly has its appeal, but are these currents conducive for fostering relationships? For building lasting friendships with our neighbors? For loving the strangers around us?

MAKING ROOM FOR HOSPITALITY

I'm convinced that to embrace biblical hospitality as a way of life one must, as Thomas Edison is often credited with saying, "fail your way to success." In other words, you have to risk opening your door, inviting people in, and seeing where God takes the relationships. Deciding to give it a try is the first step. Unfortunately,

---

[80] Dustin Willis and Brandon Clements, *The Simplest Way to Change the World: Biblical Hospitality as a Way of Life,* (Chicago, IL: Moody, 2017), 30-35.

that's the easy part. The more difficult part of embracing biblical hospitality occurs in your own life as the Spirit of God unearths your flaws and brings you face to face with your excuses and sins.

As our family began putting some of these things into practice, I can remember thinking that hospitality was destroying my life in a very literal way. Inviting people into our home interrupted my plans and my schedule. Some couples would show up early and unannounced, while others would stay much longer than expected. Opening up our home exposed our personal belongings to extra wear and tear; i.e., cracked and chipped dinnerware, broken furniture, and food and drinks spilled on the carpet. Opening our home also brought with it the invasion of space and privacy. When one of our friends informed us that she would be without housing at the end of the summer, we decided to offer her our spare bedroom. There was just one problem—my clothes were stored in her soon-to-be closet. She got her room, but my belongings were displaced, and I was inconvenienced for a season. Opening our home to others led to the depletion of food. When we first started on this journey, Lindsey and I were living on a very tight budget, but we wanted to give our guests our best in terms of food and drink. We rationalized this by saying, "We will cook a lot and use the rest as leftovers." But all too often, there were no leftovers.

I was at an extremely frustrating point in my journey. I wanted to scream. I felt like Lloyd Christmas at the climax of his frustration in the movie *Dumb and Dumber* when he said, "We've got no food! We've got no jobs! Our pets' heads are falling off!" Thankfully, we did have food, I did have a job, and no one's head was about to fall off, but I could sympathize with Lloyd's pain. I wanted to make room for hospitality, but it seemed to require too much time, too much attention, too much space, and too much food.

It's in times like those that I am extremely thankful for the local church. We had numerous people around us who constantly encouraged, supported, and challenged us in our faith, and I can honestly say that if it weren't for those people, I would've given up on loving my neighbors a long time ago. Through it all, God was teaching me that while hospitality did interrupt my schedule, people are always worth the time. He was teaching me that while hospitality did break my stuff, people are always more important than possessions. He was teaching me that while hospitality did invade my personal space, people are always craving a sense of belonging. He was teaching me that while hospitality did eat all my food, people tend to connect best over a shared meal. When God makes room for others within your heart, it's easy for you to make room for them in your home.

SQUARE FOOTAGE AND SPACE FOR OTHERS

A study conducted by the Center on Everyday Lives of Families at UCLA took a multi-year look at how Americans make use of the space within their homes.[81] By closely monitoring and map-

---

[81] Jeanne E. Arnold, Anthony P. Graesch, Enzon Ragazzini, and Elinor Ochs, *Life at Home in the Twenty-First Century: 32 Families Open Their Doors*, Los Angeles, CA: Costen Institute of Archaeology Press, 2017.

ping the whereabouts of thirty-two middle-class families, the team of researchers plotted the precise movements of these family members within their homes. While the average American home being built at the time was approximately 2,600 square feet, families only used a fraction of that space. The kitchen and family room, which included a television and a computer, were the highest-traffic areas, while the dining room, living room, and front porch were rarely, if ever, used. It's interesting that the traditional social spaces (dining room, living room, and porch), while being the larger rooms within the home, didn't yield more movement. With larger homes and additional square footage being constantly touted to entice potential homebuyers, one would expect families to actually use the space they paid for. Yet the families in the study restricted their movements, choosing to occupy smaller spaces of the home based on the primary activities of consumption and personal entertainment.

One of the most common reasons people give for not regularly practicing hospitality is they believe their house is too small. Are you ready for some good news? It's not! Your readiness for hospitality is not dependent upon your home's square footage. Concerns about where guests will sit or if people will have enough room to "stretch out" lose their clout considering that 50 percent to 60 percent of our overall square footage is hardly, if ever, used.

But what about homes during the first century? Surely homes in first century Palestine were large enough to accommodate a sizeable group of people. After all, Jesus's ministry and the early church heavily relied on households to carry out the mission for which they were sent. Would it surprise you to know that the average living room then was roughly the size of your current laundry room? Roger W. Gehring in *House Church and Mission* writes, "According to references in rabbinical texts, the dimensions of a living room in a typical house in the rural regions in Palestine at this time were about five meters square."[82] For all the non-math people out there, five meters square is almost fifty-four square feet. Clearly, the first-century Christians' hospitality toward others far surpassed the size constraints of their homes. Hospitality is thus not derived as much from physical space as it is from our love toward others and the space we make for them in our own lives. Christine Pohl writes:

> A first step in making a place for hospitality may be to make room in our hearts. Whether or not we can always find room in our houses, welcome begins with dispositions characterized by love and generosity. Hearts can be enlarged by praying that God will give us eyes to see the opportunities around us, and by putting ourselves in places where we are likely to encounter strangers in need of welcome.[83]

---

[82] Roger Gehring, *House Church and Mission: The Importance of Household Structures in Early Christianity*, (Peabody, MA: Hendrickson, 2004), 45.

[83] Christine Pohl, *Making Room: Recovering Hospitality as a Christian Tradition*, (Grand Rapids, MI: Eerdmans, 1999), 152.

CLOSE NEIGHBORS AND DISTANT RELATIONSHIPS

Several factors contributed to the rapid development of suburban housing in the 1950s and '60s. The desire to own rather than rent, to achieve a higher standard of living, and to escape the conditions of the cities all fueled consumers' longing for suburbia. Today, the suburbs, as opposed to urban and rural communities, account for the largest housing share in America, with more than 175 million people living either in the suburbs or small metros.[84] While many Americans living in suburban communities know some of their neighbors, the vast majority do not know most—much less all—of their neighbors. Even in new neighborhoods where homes are literally within a few feet of one another, neighbors can feel a sense of relational detachment despite being so physically close.

To help with this, *The Art of Neighboring* authors Runyon and Pathak created a simple tool to encourage individuals and families to reach out and build relationships with their closest neighbors. They call it "the block map," but it also goes by another name: "the chart of shame." Although not intending to "shame" anyone, this chart makes it crystal clear whether we, too, have close neighbors but distant relationships. Here's how it works: Picture a tic-tac-toe board with your house in the center. Each of the remaining eight squares represents one of your eight closest neighbors. Now here's where the fun begins. You need three pieces of information

---

[84] https://tinyurl.com/46tpxj94

to "complete" each square. The first piece of information is your neighbors' names (try to write down their first and last names). The second piece of information is something relevant about their lives that can only be gathered by speaking to them directly. You are not allowed to include anything in this step that you could gather by spying on your neighbors ("John has a blue mailbox"). The final step is to write down a piece of meaningful information about your neighbor only gathered through connecting with them personally. These answers might include their career plans or dreams after retirement, interests in hobbies, or their spiritual beliefs. Take a few moments to try it yourself and see how many squares you can complete (and no, you don't get any free points for completing your home square in the center).

Runyon and Pathak write, "After leading this exercise numerous times in many different venues, we have observed that the results are strikingly consistent: About 10 percent of people can fill out the names of all eight neighbors, line a. About 3 percent can fill out line b for every home. Less than 1 percent can fill out line c for every home."[85] Maybe you're in the top 1 percent of people who can complete the entire chart, but the reality is most of us are not. It may seem like a gargantuan leap to start talking about loving our actual neighbors when we don't even know their names, but perhaps our first step in loving our neighbors should be to start at the beginning: "Hi, my name is Justin and I live next door. I have lived in the neighborhood for years, and I apologize

---

[85] Dave Runyon and Jay Pathak, *The Art of Neighboring: Building Genuine Relationships Right Outside Your Door*, 39.

for not introducing myself sooner. What's your name?" Embrace the awkwardness and make a concerted effort to complete this chart. I have to believe there is a deep desire in each one of us to live in a neighborhood such as this, a neighborhood that is relationally rich, where we know and are known by others and where God's kingdom is tangible.

So which next step will you take? It may be to utilize the "block map" and begin learning your neighbors' names. You may start hanging out more in your front yard instead of just your backyard. Or perhaps you want to take a bigger step and open your home to those around you, sharing a dinner or a simple dessert with your closest neighbors. Whatever you decide to do, know this: With each intentional act of love, you are creating possibilities for community to blossom, for relationships to be restored, and for the gospel to be shared and experienced. That is good news for your neighborhood and for our broken and hurting world.

QUESTIONS TO CONSIDER

1. If you are honest with yourself, do you sometimes wish there was a "loophole of love"? Why can it be difficult to love our neighbors? How should the gospel change the way we perceive and treat others?

2. Do you view where you live as a "stranger-hood" or a neighborhood? Why? What can you do this week to foster a greater sense of community where you live? How can you be a blessing to those who live closest to you?

3. Have you ever experimented with biblical hospitality? If so, what was your experience like, and what did God teach you? If not, how can you begin this week?

Chapter 7

TALK WITH PEOPLE ABOUT JESUS

"Let your speech always be gracious, seasoned with salt, so
that you may know how you ought to answer each person."
Colossians 4:6

Do you remember your most embarrassing or awkward
moment? For me, one of—if not the most—awkward moments
of my life occurred in downtown Chattanooga, Tennessee. My
wife, Lindsey, and I, along with some my coworkers, had trav-
eled from Virginia to Tennessee to partner with an evangelistic
ministry for a few days. We had heard some interesting things
about the training and experiences that this ministry provided
and were sent to check it out. Part of the training involved going
into the downtown area of Chattanooga and doing what I like
to call "cold-turkey evangelism." We walked the streets for hours
stopping complete strangers and attempting to share the gospel
"cold turkey." You can imagine the range of responses we received
when we tried to stop complete strangers rushing back to work
from their lunch break, to have a conversation with those falling asleep at the bus stop, or to pray with those who were totally
uninterested. Lindsey and I were struggling to have any sort of

"success" with these encounters and decided to speak to a few more people before calling it quits. However, the most awkward instance came as Lindsey and I approached a middle-aged man in a wheelchair.

"Hi," I said. What came out next was something like, "My wife and I are here in Chattanooga sharing the love of Christ, and we wanted to know if you needed prayer?" (Opening with a question like this was how we were trained to create these types of evangelistic opportunities. Once the individual responded, we were prepared to make a beeline into our slick gospel presentation. However, for what happened next, no training would have sufficed.) "Ha!" he scoffed. "Do you even know what I am?" Not knowing what he meant, Lindsey and I glanced at each other and then back at him in silence. "I am a therianthropic anthropomegas," he said. (Pause for a second. I have met a lot of people in my life but a *therianthropic anthromegas* has never been one of them.) Next, I said what anyone else would've said in such a unique encounter: "Huh?" Through a little more questioning, we discovered that we were speaking with a man who believed he was a bona fide shapeshifter. You know—werewolves, skin-walkers, and all that kind of stuff. Lindsey and I stood there, baffled, with no idea how to respond. We offered to pray for him once more, but he refused, turned his back on us, and sped off.

I left that trip thanking God that we didn't meet him at night during a full moon but also thinking that our approach to "sharing the gospel" may have been a little amiss. This man was not only uninterested in what we had to say, he was completely turned off by our method. Hugh Halter says it this way, "Focusing on what we say without regard to how we say it doesn't work in marriage, with our kids, in politics, or in any social arrangement. So why do we think it would work with God?"[86] Perhaps our modus operandi was speaking louder than our words. Perhaps the message we had hoped to bring was overshadowed by our unwelcome technique. One thing was clear—we needed a new way of talking with people about Jesus.

WHAT IS THE GOSPEL?

If someone asked you, "What is the gospel?" what would you say? At first glance, this sounds like a simple enough question, but you'd be surprised at the range of responses I've received from professed Christians answering it. Whenever possible, I like to ask this straightforward question in a hypothetical scenario: Let's pretend a random individual comes up to you and says something like, "I've grown up going to church services and know all about serving in ministries, giving generously, and going on mission trips. But what is the gospel?" How would you answer a question like that?

Phrasing the question like that usually disrupts the cultural tendency to describe the gospel in terms of things that Christians *do* instead of who God is and what he has done in and through the person of Jesus Christ. It's a revealing question and is the

---

[86] Hugh Halter, *The Tangible Kingdom: Creating Incarnational Community*, (San Francisco, CA: Jossey- Bass, 2008), 41.

literal foundation for how and why we talk with people about Jesus in the first place.

On one occasion while interviewing a student, I got to the place where I usually pop the question and said, "So if someone came up to you and asked, 'What is the gospel?' What would you say?" Keep in mind, this particular student was spoken well of by others, volunteered his time on a weekly basis, and had even led Bible studies and small group lessons on more than one occasion. However, his answer to this question shocked me. What concerned me most about his response was what he left out: He never made a single reference to topics such as sin, holiness, repentance, grace, or faith. What's more, he never even mentioned Jesus Christ!

Sadly, this experience has not been an isolated incident. There have been countless times when the gospel has been shared in a reductionist or "small" way in relation to what the Scriptures refer to as "the Good News of the kingdom of God." Maybe you have witnessed, or even used yourself, some of the following variations of a "small" gospel:

- A "small" gospel is one that's primarily focused on the afterlife.
  - o While the afterlife is a major concern, the gospel has got to be more than your "get-out-of-jail-free card" or your "ticket to heaven." The gospel has massive implications for your life right here and right now.

- A "small" gospel is one that's presented as a sales pitch.
  - o While tools for sharing can be useful at times, the gospel has got to be more than a few spiritual laws, theological points, or key phrases used to get people to make a quick spiritual transaction.

- A "small" gospel is one that sounds like bad news.
  - o While there is an element of "bad news" about the overall human condition resulting from sin, the gospel is much more than a cosmic guilt trip.

To help answer the question, "What is the gospel?" perhaps we need what Caesar Kalinowski often refers to as a "bigger gospel." Here is what he means:

> So many of us have believed in a tiny, truncated gospel. It is primarily about sin management, behavioral modification and someday getting out of here and going to heaven. But looking at the full story of God, and the bigger gospel found throughout all of scripture, we see this: You were created in the image of a loving and gracious God, and destined for an eternal relationship with him. Though it is true that you have rebelled against God, thinking you could create an identity for yourself, one where you are lord over your own life, God himself came on a rescue mission to restore all people, places,

and things back to relationship with him (including you), back to the way he originally designed it to be. There is a day coming when he will once again walk and live and dwell with us in a city that is like a beautiful garden forever and ever.[87]

The gospel of the kingdom of God, or the Good News, is a story that spans the entirety of the Bible. And this grand story, much like major acts in a theatrical performance or like musical movements in a symphony, can be summarized in four thematic words. They are as follows:

1. **Creation:** God has always existed and will always exist (Gen. 1:1; John 1:1-5). God is holy and always does what is perfect and good—it's in his nature! In the beginning of the Bible, God chose to create all things, including humanity. He created man and woman in a special way—in his own image (Gen. 1:26-28). He placed them in a beautiful garden where they experienced perfect relationships with creation, one another, and God himself.

2. **Fall:** As the story unfolds, the first humans (Adam and Eve) chose to rebel against God's command (Gen. 2:16). They decided to live their own way instead of God's (Gen. 3:6). The Bible calls this sin. Since God does not allow sin to be in his presence, Adam and

---

[87] Caesar Kalinowski, *Bigger Gospel: Learning to Speak, Live, and Enjoy the Good News in Every Area of Life*, (Missio Publishing: 2017), 41-42.

Eve were sent away from the Garden and were subject to the difficulties of life—things like sickness,
pain, and death. Their perfect relationships with creation, one another, and God had been fractured by
sin. As time went on, sin spread to all people (Gen.
5:5-6), and all the generations that followed lived in a
sin-fractured world, choosing their own way instead
of God's way.

3. **Redemption:** God chose to make a special agreement
(a covenant) with a man named Abram (Genesis 12).
God said that he would use Abram and his family
to be a blessing to the world by showing everyone
what it looked like to once again live according to
the good and perfect ways of God. He gave Abram
descendants, favor, and land as his family grew into
a nation (Israel). As this nation matured, they struggled to love God and follow his ways (Judges 21:25).
They frequently chased after the things of the world
(wealth, power, possessions, people) instead of living wholeheartedly for God. Because of their sin,
this nation was sent into exile (similar to how Adam
and Eve were sent out of the Garden) and wound
up a defeated nation of slaves. Despite their failure,
God would still be true to his original covenant with
Abram. One day in the future, a descendant from
Israel would be born who would return things to
the way they were intended to be (Jer. 31:31; Ezek.

36:22-28). Then there were roughly 400 years of silence. As the New Testament opens, Israel was under the rule and governance of a national super-power—Rome. An angel, sent from God, spoke to a young Israelite woman named Mary. The angel told her that she would give birth to a special child whose name was to be Jesus. This birth was supernatural, and Jesus would be God's Son, the one who would save his people from their sins (Matt. 1:21). Jesus was born and lived the perfect life, always choosing to live God's way. He called people to follow him to experience the "kingdom of God," showing people how to, once again, live under God's rule and reign. In order to rescue humanity from their sin problem, Jesus was crucified on their behalf, taking in his own body the punishment for sin that humanity really deserved. God accepted Jesus's sacrifice in place of humanity's, and by believing in him (John 3:16) humanity could once again be at peace with God. But the story doesn't end there. After Jesus gave up his life on the cross, he was placed in a tomb and three days later came back to life! This was witnessed by his followers and more than 500 other people (1 Cor. 15:3-8). Jesus then ascended into heaven to be with God the Father (Acts 1:6-11) and sent the Holy Spirit to dwell in those who believe in him (Acts 2). The Holy Spirit dwells inside Christ followers and helps them to walk and live in the ways of God.

4. **Restoration:** This was the beginning of what the Bible calls the church. The church is a community of Christ followers imbued with the Spirit of God who live in mission with God in the world. The church is to live according to God's ways, and together their lives show the world what the kingdom of God is like and will be like in the future. Jesus promised that one day soon he would return to earth to bring the kingdom of God in its complete fullness. At that time, he will restore everything to the way it was intended to be—a world with no more evil, sin, or rebellion. A world with no more sickness, pain, or death. It will be utter paradise, just like it was in the beginning.

This is the "bigger" gospel. You have to admit, this story is much more compelling than any of the "small" gospel examples. What if we could all learn to speak this story into every aspect of our lives? What if we knew this story so well that it began to flavor all of our conversations? I believe that we can. With practice and intentionality and help from the Spirit, we can learn to share a bigger gospel that is more comprehensive, that is more in touch with this life and the next, and that sounds like "good news" from the get-go.

GOD'S STORY AND OUR STORY

So how, specifically, can we use this bigger gospel in our everyday conversations as we talk with people about Jesus? Using this story as a framework can be one of the best ways to get to know others and simultaneously speak gospel truths into each other's lives. Here is what I mean: Just as the story of the Bible starts with creation, every person's life story has a beginning. Just as the story of the Bible speaks about the Fall, every person has experienced brokenness. Just as the story of the Bible anticipates redemption, every person is pursuing betterment in some measure. Just as the story of the Bible longs for restoration, every person hopes for future blessings.

Every person has a literal beginning (birth), but they have other kinds of "beginnings" in life as well—starting a new job or career, getting married, having children, moving to another state. In all these instances, people are beginning something new, and they have underlying beliefs about who or what got them to where they are in life. When talking to others about Jesus, it's important to discern whether these underlying beliefs are positive or negative. Does the person blame others for their situation? Do they believe their life has been negatively affected by a difficult upbringing or other influences? On the flip side, the person may unashamedly credit themselves with their success or standing. In either case, when people discuss their beginnings, they are really answering the question "How did I get here?"

Similarly, everyone has experienced brokenness. In a perfect world, everyone would experience love and happiness, but in our sin-fractured world, pain is unfortunately the common denominator. Just like Adam and Eve in the Garden (see Genesis 3), we are all looking for someone to blame for the brokenness we experience in the world. Talk with anyone, whatever their religious convictions, and they will say that they have an undeniable sense that the world is not as it should be.

- Unloving families and social injustices.

- Loneliness and abandonment.

- Unexplained illness and death.

- Murder and hatred.

- Greed, lies, and corruption.

The list could go on and on. When listening to other people's stories, it's important to interpret how they process the brokenness of the world and the brokenness of their own lives. Their answers will reveal their beliefs about the question "Why are things this way?"

It is only natural to look for betterment in a broken world. After all, when most encounter a problem, they search for a solution. Everyone, whether they say so or not, is searching for someone or something that will bring betterment to their life. Some may search for betterment through relationships, believing the solution to their life will be found in romance or marriage. Others may go the self-improvement route, pursuing higher education, personal enrichment, or worldly success. Some may rely on politics, believing government to be the solution. Whatever the case may be, everyone is seeking a solution to the brokenness they see on a daily basis and have experienced in their own life. As this portion of their story is shared, it will reveal their beliefs about the question "What can make life better?"

This leads to the final aspect of our stories: blessings. Blessings reveal our hope for the future. Blessings explain what we believe will result from our search for betterment. Here's an example: Say a person is pursuing betterment through relationships. The blessings they hope that relationship will provide may be greater happiness, a more fulfilling life, and personal security. If you were to close your eyes and picture an ideal world, what would come to mind? Whatever it is, those are blessings. When sharing our personal stories, many times we allude to our hopes for the future (peace, love, security, equality, justice). This final portion of their story reveals their beliefs about the question "What will life be like when all is well?"

The chart below helps to bring all this together by showing how the gospel story's framework is woven into our personal

The Story of the Gospel	The Story of Our Lives	Answers the Question
Creation	*Beginnings*	*How did I get here?*
Fall	*Brokenness*	*Why are things this way?*
Redemption	*Betterment*	*What can make life better?*
Restoration	*Blessings*	*What will life be like when all is well?*

stories, including shared foundational questions each aspect helps to answer.

As you begin to rehearse the story of the gospel in your own life, you will begin to hear how others use this framework to tell their personal stories. This framework applies to Christ followers and to those who do not yet follow Jesus. As each of us shares our own story, this framework establishes common ground on which we can relate to one another. While it's true that not everyone has experienced redemption in Christ, you will be hard-pressed to find someone who is not pursuing some measure of betterment in life. The question is, to whom or to what are we looking to make life better? Intentionally using this framework to talk with others about Jesus creates an ongoing conversation that shares the truths of the gospel in a gracious and life-giving way. As others share, use this framework to discern what "good news" would sound like to them and how the gospel can speak into their personal stories and life situations.

BEGINNINGS, BROKENNESS, BETTERMENT, BLESSINGS (AN EXAMPLE)

When friends get together, especially when they are first getting to know one another, it doesn't take long for someone to share a story. Before you know it, the whole group gets caught up in story-swapping. I am captivated by a good story, as we all are, and have come to realize that our lives are often reflections of the primary stories we tell ourselves and others. On one particular occasion, while we sat around swapping stories, one of our new friends began sharing the story of her life. As I listened, I was amazed at how her story perfectly followed the progression of beginnings, brokenness, betterment, and blessings.

As she began, she mentioned that she grew up poor and that often her family struggled to make ends meet. Money was always a source of frustration within her household. Her clothes were frequently too small and out of style, showing signs of being handed down from sibling to sibling. On top of that, food was scarce. Memories of going hungry or eating half-prepared meals while rushing from place to place were all too common as she talked about her humble beginnings.

As heartbreaking as these conditions may sound, these beginnings were not her greatest source of brokenness. As she continued to be vulnerable with our groups, her relationship with her parents clearly caused the deepest pain. As the family finances worsened, so did her relationship with her parents. She mentioned that she was repeatedly put down and made to feel like she had to prove herself to be loved. If she stepped out of line or made a mistake, she was slapped, often in the face. Repeated name-calling and harsh punishment left her internally defeated, and she began to wonder if she was to blame for the brokenness in her life.

At some point, she decided she had had enough. She was tired of her life and determined to work her way out of her situation. Intellectually gifted and already receiving good grades in school, she devised a simple yet effective plan—education would be her escape. With a little more focus and effort, she would excel, and a new purpose began to emerge in her life. Giving her all to education would ensure that she got into a good university, which would lead to securing a decent job and, hopefully, becoming financially independent along the way. She resolved to *be* nothing like and *live* nothing like her past, and she chose education as her path forward.

This idea led her to pursue her current job, and she began to express her hopes for what her future would bring and what she could provide for her future family. The wealth she was experiencing was completely different than her dark past, and she hinted that she fully expected it would bring her peace, security, and happiness. By securing a good job with a consistent salary, she would finally be given the respect she deserved and experience the fulfillment she so desperately craved.

Did you hear it? The story of her life, while drastically different than the story of the gospel, mirrors it perfectly. This story naturally progressed from beginnings, to brokenness, to betterment, and finally to blessings. As we listen closely and compassionately, we will be able to discern what people are believing in to rescue, restore, and redeem their lives. The chart on the next page that shows the underlying beliefs in this story.

The gospel of Jesus Christ offers a better story than the ones we tell and create for ourselves. It is the true story and is good news to those who have been searching for answers within themselves and the world. Knowing the story of the gospel and using it as a framework for interacting with others can help us speak truth into people's lives, producing conversations that open doors for

The Story of our Lives	Answers the Question	Example Story
Beginnings	*How did I get here?*	*Humble upbringing, experiencing want*
Brokenness	*Why are things this way?*	*Lack of finances, unhealthy relationships*
Betterment	*What can make life better?*	*Education, secure job, wealth*
Blessings	*What will life be like when all is well?*	*Peace, security, respect from others*

talking with others about Jesus. As the apostle Paul reminds us, "Let your speech always be gracious, seasoned with salt, so that you may know how you ought to answer each person."[88]

CONVERSATIONS OR PRESENTATIONS?

It used to be that information was enough. One could share a clear and logical presentation and expect the listeners to respond positively to what was communicated. After all, information found to be true ought to be believed—or so it once was. This is

---

[88] Colossians 4:6

how I was taught to share the gospel. I was trained in a method of evangelism that required a memorized presentation. Each week, our local church's evangelism team got in our cars and paid a visit to the guests who had attended the previous week's church service. A decent night "doing evangelism" would consist of us knocking on doors and asking people a few key questions about their spiritual beliefs. But a great night would involve us sharing our memorized presentations and conversing with people about them afterward. But things are changing so much in our cultural context that our strategies have to change as well.

At one point in time, the cultural majority in America would have generally agreed with the basic tenets and assumptions of Christianity: the authority of the Bible, the deity of Christ, and the exclusivity of the gospel. One would have been able to give a gospel presentation to a listener who was actually familiar with the majority of the key words and concepts used, making it fairly simple to have a meaningful conversation about faith. Today, this is not the case. We live in a post-Christian context in which the majority of people do not adhere to a biblical worldview, regularly attend a church, read the Bible, or want to associate with any religion. Try sharing an old-school gospel presentation in this post-Christian context, and you are more likely to get blank stares and confused looks than you are people turning their lives over to Jesus.

Sam Chan, in his book *Evangelism in a Skeptical World*, describes how this shift in culture ought to change how the church talks with others about Jesus. In the past, the church used this logical sequence in sharing the gospel:

Truth, Belief, Praxis

- This is true.

- If it's true, then you must believe it.

- If you believe it, now you must live it.[89]

In other words, the church was really good at sharing the truth through a presentation, asking the listener to believe the truth by making a decision, and then inviting them to live out their faith by changing their lifestyle. However, he suggests that culture has totally flipped, and since it has, the church's strategy must as well. The more culturally appropriate flow is as follows:

Praxis, Belief, Truth

- The Christian life is livable.

- If it's livable, then it's also believable.

- If it's believable, then it's also true.[90]

Notice that in our current culture, the "front door" of talking with others about Jesus is built on a relationship. Relationships naturally require ongoing conversations and sharing life with one another. Chan summarizes it this way:

> Therefore, evangelism to postmoderns requires a lifestyle change. We need our Christian friends to

---

[89] Sam Chan, *Evangelism in a Skeptical World: How to Make the Unbelievable News About Jesus More Believable*, (Grand Rapids, MI: Zondervan, 2018), 125.

[90] *Ibid.*

become friends with our non-Christian friends. We need to be part of the same community. And then our non-Christian friends can see how the Christian life works. They will discover it is livable. And if they see that, they will see that it's believable. And if they see that, they might also acknowledge that it's true. But this will happen only if we live with our non-Christian friends. Not just visit them. Not just go out with them. But live among them so that they are part of our closest network of friends, and we are part of their closest network of friends.[91]

Does this mean the church should never give a gospel presentation? Absolutely not! Memorizing a scripted gospel presentation can help organize your thoughts and, when you're given the opportunity, help you communicate biblical truth in a concise way. But it does mean that the church needs to cultivate new habits for talking with people about Jesus. Learning to have ongoing gospel conversations with others models the patient and gracious life that Christ displayed while he lived and walked this earth. By living S.E.N.T., the church can once again talk with others about Jesus in a culturally compelling and Christ-centered way.

As you go throughout your life in the days ahead, I challenge you to begin a gospel conversation with someone you know. It may be as simple as asking an intentional question and listening

---

[91] Chan, *Evangelism in a Skeptical World*, 125

to their story with a genuine interest. Remember, you are not trying to convert someone; only God can transform a life. May our focus be on obedience—sharing the Good News as we live S.E.N.T. in the world.

QUESTIONS TO CONSIDER

1. Which of the "small" gospels have you heard or experienced most often? (Refer back to the three small gospels within this chapter on pages 127 and 128 for reference.) What questions, if any, did those variations leave with you? In what ways do you need to adopt a "bigger" gospel?

2. In what ways does thinking through the gospel as a story (creation, fall, redemption, restoration) help you understand the Bible's bigger, overall message?

3. Challenge: Try sharing the gospel as a story (creation, fall, redemption, restoration) with a few trusted friends or your small group. Learning to share and speak with fluency takes practice and time, so be sure to encourage one another along the way. (PS: If you need some help, go back to the four "missional movements" of chapter 1. Those are another useful tool for sharing the gospel as a story.)

PART III
TOGETHER

Chapter 8

LIVING S.E.N.T. TOGETHER

"Iron sharpens iron, and one man sharpens another."
Solomon (Proverbs 27:17)

"In the Bible, the real test of what you know is how you live."
Mike Frost

Information alone will not change you. Nor will you turn into an everyday missionary who lives S.E.N.T. just from reading this book. Think about it: Today's church has access to the most Bible information in history and almost instantaneous access to myriad sermons, Bible studies, podcasts, books, blogs, curriculums, and conferences, yet people are still struggling in their own spiritual formation. People often seek new information when attempting to incorporate a new healthy habit into their lives or defeat an old, undesirable one. B.J. Fogg, the founder of the Behavioral Design Lab at Stanford University, calls this the "Information-Action Fallacy." He writes, "Many products and programs—and well-meaning professionals—set out to educate people as a way to change them. 'If people just knew the facts, they would change!'"[92] This fallacy holds that humans function much like machines, and if we download new data we can change our fundamental operating systems. The hope is that by consuming copious amounts of information, something will stick and lead us down the path of transformation. Often, instead of producing change, this approach has the opposite effect, leading people to constantly search for the "newest" and "latest" rather than applying what they already know to be true.

Dan White Jr. writes in *The Church as Movement*: "Merely transferring spiritual information can inoculate us to on-the-ground practice. Practice is being formed and informed by the bumps, bruises, and baptism of application. To embody our beliefs and work them out in real-time practice is at the soul of being a Jesus follower."[93] Jesus fully expected this of his followers and constantly gave them outlets for application in real time to "try on" and "try out" his kingdom teachings. His teachings, while including much information, were decisively application-oriented. In other words, he encouraged his followers to not only hear and receive relevant information but to do it, apply it, obey it, and truly live it.

In order to begin living S.E.N.T. lives together, we need to move beyond mere knowledge acquisition and push ourselves

[92] B.J. Fogg, *Tiny Habits: The Small Changes That Change Everything*, (New York, NY: Houghton Mifflin Harcourt, 2020), 4.

[93] J.R. Woodward and Dan White Jr., *The Church as Movement: Starting and Sustaining Missional-Incarnational Communities*, (Downers Grove, IL: IVP Books, 2016), 91.

into the space of application and experimentation. Trying on and trying out new missional habits is the path to incorporating them into our daily routines and embedding them into our lives— making them not just what we do but also who we are. But we are certainly not expected to do this alone. We do this together.

Together, in the power of the Holy Spirit.

Together, in partnership with other believers.

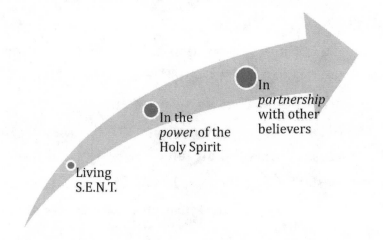

YOU CANNOT DO THIS ALONE

For roughly three years, Jesus's disciples watched him perform many miracles—healing the sick, restoring sight to the blind, casting out demons, and raising the dead. They saw him multiply paltry amounts of food to feed thousands of people. They witnessed him silence a raging storm and calm a wild sea. They saw him carry his cross to Calvary, give up his life, and then three days later come back to life! They knew the all facts about Jesus and probably could have written a textbook's worth of information about his earthly ministry. But instead of getting right to work spreading the Good News of the Kingdom, Jesus told them to wait (Luke 24:48-49).

The final words Jesus spoke to his followers before ascending into heaven are recorded in the first few verses of the book of Acts. He says in Acts 1:8, "But you will receive power when the Holy Spirit has come upon you, and you will be my witnesses in Jerusalem and in all Judea and Samaria, and to the end of the earth." The promised Spirit would grace them with supernatural power that would strengthen their troubled hearts, embolden their timid spirits, and fill their empty mouths with the right words. The Spirit would equip them to live out their calling from Jesus. It would be the Spirit of God, not the disciples themselves, that performed the supernatural work of salvation in the lives of men and women. The disciples were simply spiritual conduits, instruments used by God to alert the world to his universal reign.

In other words, the disciples' witness was predicated on their receiving of the Holy Spirit.

Jesus didn't want them witnessing to the Good News in their own power, and he doesn't want you to do so either. He didn't want them to derive their sense of confidence from their own ability or "know-how." Instead, Jesus asked them to wait until they received power. To fulfill their calling to be his witnesses, they would need to live S.E.N.T. together in the power of the Holy Spirit. We get to do the same.

If we hope to have any sort of missional effectiveness by living S.E.N.T., we will do so through the power of the Holy Spirit.

Instead of you working for God, it will be God working through you to accomplish his work in and around you. Trying to live S.E.N.T. apart from the Spirit will leave you spinning your wheels as you attempt to gain traction in something that only God can do. As we daily commune with God and walk in obedience to his commands, we can stay alert to how the Spirit would have us engage those around us.

Where missional effectiveness comes through living S.E.N.T. in the power of the Holy Spirit, missional endurance is fostered by living S.E.N.T. in partnership with other believers. Since integrating missional habits into our lives will take time and effort, it becomes essential to surround ourselves with others who will keep us accountable. Try to live S.E.N.T. alone, and you will likely find yourself tapping out early—especially when things begin to get hard or inconvenient.

My suggestion would be to surround yourself with two or three people who also are working to integrate these missional habits into their lives. Schedule regular meetings to review the Live S.E.N.T. Reflection (Appendix A). This reflection is a tool that will not only keep a record of how you lived S.E.N.T. during the week, but will also prompt you and the group to pray, asking the Spirit to reveal your next steps as you continue to live S.E.N.T. Completing this reflection and meeting with this group will encourage you to continue living like a missionary, even when things become difficult and inconvenient—and trust me, they will! Life happens. Schedules get mixed up. And sometimes you just have an "off" week. But even though there are instances when you don't live S.E.N.T., these groups will serve as places of grace, supporting you every step of the way. If one week you don't compete every section in the Live S.E.N.T. Reflection, the group won't beat you up or make you feel guilty. Instead, as you share honestly about your life, the group will pray for you and encourage you to press on in what God is doing around you.

Remember, living S.E.N.T. is fun and rewarding! Partnering with God in what he is doing in us, through us, and around us is the adventure of a lifetime.

QUESTIONS TO CONSIDER

1. Have you ever fallen victim to the "Information-Action Fallacy"? If so, what did you learn from the experience? In your own words, how have you seen applying Jesus's teachings transform your life?

2. Which do you believe will be easier for you: living S.E.N.T. in the power of the Spirit or in partnership with others? Why? What steps can you take to help you grow in living S.E.N.T. together?

3. Who in your life would be a good fit to invite into a live S.E.N.T. group? Challenge: Begin praying about a few people you would like to ask to join you in this group. After you finish this book, reach out to them and see what they say.

CHAPTER 9

WHEREVER YOU ARE

"We cannot all do great things.
But we can do small things with great love."

Mother Teresa

Michelle had called Lindsey (my wife) earlier that day to tell her she would be stopping by the house to drop off some old baby clothes that she no longer needed for her kids. With three children under the age of five at the time, Lindsey and I were happy to take them off her hands! We were busy tackling some chores around the house when Michelle arrived. We had gotten to know Michelle and her family better over the past year, and she felt comfortable letting herself in. I was washing the dishes and Lindsey was folding some laundry while we all talked. As we settled into the conversation, Lindsey asked, "How are you and Mike doing?" A few moments later, I heard Lindsey call my name.

"Justin!"

"Yes?" I responded over the sound of running water.

"Did you not hear what Michelle just said?"

As I looked up, Michelle had tears in her eyes. I quickly turned off the faucet and dried my hands as I walked into the living room. Michelle repeated herself saying, "Mike and I are not doing too well. We are getting a divorce." We asked her if she would like to stay for lunch and her visit, which would have normally only lasted a few minutes, turned into a few hours. As we ate, we listened to Michelle's story and tried to understand as best we could. We prayed for Michelle and her marriage, reminding her of the gospel and that the Lord specializes in repairing broken relationships and can bring healing into even the most impossible of situations. After many more questions, talking, and even more listening, Lindsey gave Michelle our spare house key, letting her know that she could use our home however she needed in the days and months ahead. We hugged Michelle as she left and then continued to pray for her even after she was gone.

I share this story only to illustrate that opportunities to live S.E.N.T. don't always occur when we expect them. You can't schedule living S.E.N.T. when it's convenient. Living like everyday, ordinary missionaries means that we are to always be ready to serve others as God in Christ served us. This means that our time, our food, our space, and our very lives are constantly available to be the means through which we bless others. These S.E.N.T. habits are habits of sacrifice and generosity, peacemaking and humility, love and compassion. You, too, will have pages full of stories about how the Lord will work through you as you live S.E.N.T. in your household, neighborhood, and community.

What part will you play?

Whom has he sent you to already?

What are you waiting for?

Live S.E.N.T.

APPENDIX A
LIVE S.E.N.T. REFLECTION

See People like Jesus

(Goal: Meet three new people this week, one of whom is not a member of my church.)

Who did I meet for the first time, reconnect with, or see differently this week?

_____	_____
_____	_____
_____	_____
_____	_____

How can I begin to intentionally pray for each person?

_____

_____

_____

_____

Eat with People like Jesus

(Goal: Eat with three people this week, one of whom is not a member of my church.)

Who did I grab coffee with, get lunch with, or have over for dinner this week?

_____   _____

_____   _____

_____   _____

_____   _____

Who is the Spirit asking me to contact or reach out to next week?

_____

_____

_____

_____

Neighbor People like Jesus

(Goal: Take one "next step" with a literal neighbor this week.)

Who did I take a "next step" with this week?

_____   _____

_____   _____

_____   _____

Who is the Spirit prompting me to bless in my neighborhood, workplace, or community next week?

_____

_____

_____

_____

Talk with People About Jesus

(Goal: Have one gospel conversation this week.)

With whom did I have a gospel conversation this week?

_____   _____

_____   _____

_____   _____

_____   _____

How can I continue that conversation with them in the future?

_____

_____

_____

APPENDIX B
SIX-WEEK SMALL GROUP GUIDE

HOW TO USE THE GUIDE

This six-week small group guide is adaptable to any kind of group: missional community, small group, Sunday school class, life group, church staff, etc. It could be used as a personal study, but I strongly encourage you to go through this material with a few people who also are being intentional about living S.E.N.T. and learning to incorporate these missional rhythms into their daily lives.

Each week, the small group guide has a reading assignment. Ideally, every participant will have read the corresponding chapter and come prepared to share and encourage others (this is not required but will dramatically benefit the group). From there, follow the outline, ask the reflection questions, read the selected quotes, open the Bible in the "Deeper Look" section, and conclude with the discussion questions.

After completing this six-week guide, you may want to meet regularly with two or three people for encouragement and accountability as you integrate these habits into your life. My prayer is that this would be a supportive resource to you as you embrace what it means to live like a missionary wherever you are.

TIPS FOR USING THE GUIDE

- **Pray:** This should really go without saying, but pray for your group. Pray early and pray often. Pray before your group even meets, while your group is meeting, and at the conclusion of your gathering time. If prayer is not already a regular rhythm of your group, you will be amazed how it transforms your time together. You don't have to do this alone. Ask around and mobilize others to pray with you.

- **Leave Space for People to Respond:** It is natural to try to fill empty conversational space, but resist the urge to do so—especially if you are the facilitator or leading the group. Remember that group members are often chewing on lesson ideas, processing what you have said, and formulating their responses, all of which take time. Be confident in your question and be patient while the Spirit prompts people to speak up.

- **Be Transparent:** People respect authenticity and "realness." Even if what you share is a failure or a struggle, be transparent with your group. Your transparency can inspire others to share something personal, leading to better discussions and more opportunities for growth and encouragement.

- **Don't Be the Expert:** As the facilitator or group leader, many may look to you for the "right" answers. You don't have to have the right answers. In fact, it's best that you don't. If you are constantly being asked for the "correct" answers, try re-asking the question. This will free you up from having to be the expert while also granting other members of the group an opportunity to speak up.

- **Begin by Reviewing the Previous Week's Discussion Questions:** Aside from week one, each subsequent week has Discussion Questions that will be a great starting point for your group. Start by reviewing the questions and asking the group what life changes they have made in light of the content.

SMALL GROUP GUIDE: WEEK 1

BEFORE GATHERING:

- Have everyone read *Live S.E.N.T.* chapters 1 and 2.

REFLECTION:

- How do you respond to what C.H. Spurgeon said at the beginning of chapter 2? ("Every Christian is either a missionary or an imposter.") Do you agree with this? Why or why not?

- If you began to see yourself as a missionary sent by Jesus, how would this change the way you interact with your family, friends, neighbors, coworkers, or classmates?

QUOTES:

"From Jesus, then, flows the mission of the church until he comes again. His final words to his disciples and action form a sending, a commission, a mandate. Those who are disciples of Jesus today are to be like the disciples of Jesus in the Gospels—called to be with him and to go in his name to do his work, to the ends of the earth and until the end of the world. Churches, then, are to be communities around the world, planted, nurtured, and connected through ministries of sending, going, and supporting—for the sake of the name of Christ and the truth of the gospel."[94] (From page 39)

So, what does this have to do with you and your local church? Everything! If you are a follower of Christ, that means you—and everyone in your local church—is a full-time minister of the gospel who has been commissioned by Jesus to live a "sent" life. And if you really think about it, that changes everything. It changes how we gather as the church. It changes how we scatter as the church. This means that we need to interpret our neighborhoods, workplaces, and cities as places to which we have been sent. This means that we need to interpret our social networks, neighbors, and communities as people to whom we have been sent. We don't *have* to do this. We *get* to do this! (From page 40)

A DEEPER LOOK:

- Read John 17.

- Notice verses 11, 16, and 18. Jesus said of his followers that they are "in the world," they are "not of the world," and they have been "sent into the world."

- What does each of these statements mean? Does your current lifestyle agree with these three statements?

[94] Christopher Wright, *The Mission of God's People*, (Grand Rapids, MI: Zondervan, 2010), 221.

GROUP DISCUSSION:

- Which of the four missional movements within Scripture (missional family, missional nation, missional Savior, missional church) was most helpful in seeing the bigger story of God's mission throughout history?

- What personal changes do you need to make for living S.E.N.T. to become a lifestyle for you?

SMALL GROUP GUIDE: WEEK 2

BEFORE GATHERING:

- Have everyone read *Live S.E.N.T.* chapter 3.

REFLECTION:

- At first glance, which of the four S.E.N.T. habits resonates most with you and why? Which one does the opposite?

- Challenge: Conduct a weekly audit by focusing on the S.E.N.T. habits. Which ones do you naturally do? Which ones do you naturally avoid?

QUOTES:

In whatever measure these practices already exist in your life, the good news is this: you can change. In fact, the gospel challenges every one of us to change. It challenges us to change in our whole lives, not just in a component or section of it. Thus the entirety of our lives, not just one day of the week, is a reflection of our faith in Christ (how we invest our time, how we interact with and relate to others, how we manage our possessions, how we conduct ourselves in our vocations, how we choose to raise our children). If our only "Christian" habits are going to church services on Sundays and saying "grace" before meals, how will the world come to know the Good News of the gospel? (From page 48)

Can you imagine cultivating meaningful relationships with 156 people in a year? Having 156 meals
fueled by gospel intentionality? Taking fifty-two
"next steps" with your closest neighbors? Having
fifty-two gospel conversations? How about a local
church that purposefully connects with 15,600
nonmembers in a year? Shares over 15,000 gospel-saturated meals with others, loves their community in thousands of tangible ways, and shares
the Good News thousands and thousands of times
a year? Just the idea of a person, a small group, or
a local church living S.E.N.T. for one year could
change entire households, neighborhoods, and cities with the gospel! What are you waiting for? Let's
live S.E.N.T. (From page 51)

A DEEPER LOOK:

- The word "habit" only appears once in the New
  Testament. It is found in Hebrews 10. Read
  Hebrews 10:24-25.

- The author of Hebrews encourages his readers to
  not develop the poor habit of "neglecting to meet
  together." The opposite is implied: cultivate the
  "good" habit of meeting with one another regularly.

- In light of this passage, what is the role of
  community and accountability in forming and
  cultivating positive, good habits?

GROUP DISCUSSION:

- As you think about changing some of your habits, which of the S.E.N.T. habits will be easiest to adopt? Which will be most difficult?

SMALL GROUP GUIDE: WEEK 3

BEFORE GATHERING:

- Have everyone read *Live S.E.N.T.* chapter 4.

REFLECTION:

- Which category, place, people, or persuasion presents the largest barrier to you in being able to see people like Jesus? What steps can you take to change that?

- Quickly take Hans Finzel's "peoplework versus paperwork" test. What is your default reaction? What can you do to begin viewing others more as opportunities than interruptions?

- Try to memorize the three practical ways to see people like Jesus: make eye contact, use their names, give a genuine compliment. This week, keep a journal of how doing these things changes you and your interactions with others.

QUOTES:

How often do we let the categories of place, people, and persuasion keep us from seeing others the way Jesus sees them? It is so much safer to avoid "that part of town." It is so much more comfortable to hang out with people "like us." It is so much easier to talk with those who share our worldview, our values, and our political views. But is that what

Jesus has sent us to do? Has Jesus sent us into the world to be people who always choose what is safe, comfortable, and easy? If Jesus really has called his Church to live S.E.N.T., then his Church is also expected to do the hard, missionary work of crossing categories so that we can truly see the individual. (From page 64)

The most important thing is to listen to the Holy Spirit's guidance in these things. If the Spirit prompts you to meet someone, then do it! If he prompts you to compliment someone you meet, then do it! But don't force these things just so you can say that you did them or to check them off some list. These are simply avenues for relational connection that much of society has lost. The majority of people do not make eye contact. The majority of people do not take the time to use, let alone learn, your name. The majority of people do not compliment one another. As followers of Christ, we should strive to make relational connections with the people God puts into our path and truly see the inherent value of those around us. (From page 76)

A DEEPER LOOK:

- Read Luke 7:11-18.

- Discuss the various ways that Jesus "saw" others in this story. Discuss the boundaries he was willing to cross to demonstrate the coming kingdom. (Hint:

Jesus's compassion for the woman leads him to take action in various ways.)

GROUP DISCUSSION:

- What stops you from "seeing others like Jesus"? Preoccupation? A sense of hurry? Deadlines and to-do lists?

- How can you begin to take note of others around you this week? In what ways can you begin to listen to the Spirit's guidance as you go about your daily routines?

SMALL GROUP GUIDE: WEEK 4

BEFORE GATHERING:
- Have everyone read *Live S.E.N.T.* chapter 5.

REFLECTION:
- Think back on your life. Which meals have been your favorite? Apart from the delicious food, what made them so special?

- How do Jesus's radically inclusive eating habits challenge your life? Are there people whom you have unknowingly, or intentionally, excluded? What are you going to do about it?

QUOTES:

Thus, is it fair to think of Jesus as a party animal? While he certainly ate and drank frequently throughout his ministry, sharing meals with others was not an end in and of itself. Jesus leveraged the meal for the mission on which he was sent, calling people to him and challenging them to follow him with their whole lives. We, too, can leverage the shared meal for mission, creating opportunities to develop deeper relationships with others and invite them to follow Christ. (From page 84)

Jesus's radical inclusion stemmed from his contagious holiness. He wasn't afraid of others' moral impurity rubbing off on him. His contact with others doesn't result in his defilement but in their restoration. His table fellowship with others doesn't result in a cross-contamination of immorality or wickedness. Rather, his gracious presence with the spiritually wayward and impure steadily wooed them toward the call of discipleship, toward leaving their former way of life, toward taking up their cross and following him. (From page 89)

A DEEPER LOOK:

- Read Luke 5:32; 7:47-50; 19:10; 22:14-16.

- The setting in each of these passages is a shared meal. Jesus and those around him were most likely in a reclined position around the table. How does Jesus's posture change your perception of some of his most famous words?

- Does the informality of Jesus's posture as he speaks these powerful words seem odd? Comforting? Why?

- Does his example in these passages encourage you to have deep/difficult/spiritual conversations? Why or why not?

GROUP DISCUSSION:

- Which of the following—being present, asking questions, or limiting technology—do you need to work on the most? What small change can you make to help foster these habits?

- How can you creatively begin to invite others into your life through meals this week? Does "eating with people like Jesus" always need to be elaborate, or can it be simple?

SMALL GROUP GUIDE: WEEK 5

BEFORE GATHERING:

- Have everyone read *Live S.E.N.T.* chapter 6.

REFLECTION:

- If you are honest with yourself, do you sometimes wish there was a "loophole of love"? Why can it be difficult to love our neighbors? How should the gospel change the way we perceive and treat others?

- Do you view where you live as a "stranger-hood" or a neighborhood? Why? What can you do this week to foster a greater sense of community where you live? How can you be a blessing to those who live closest to you?

QUOTES:

Maybe you've lived in your neighborhood for years and have never been intentional about meeting your neighbors. Or perhaps you just moved to a new city or subdivision where the busyness of unpacking and getting settled has taken priority over meeting the folks around you. Whatever the case may be, it's never too late to start because our immediate mission field rarely changes: it's the street on which we live. As Christ followers, we must see that God has called us to embody the gospel on the very street where we live and among the very people we call neighbors. Loving your neighbors begins with this understanding: you have been sent to live in such a way that makes the kingdom of God tangible in your neighborhood. (From page 105)

Through it all, God was teaching me that while hospitality did interrupt my schedule, people are always worth the time. He was teaching me that while hospitality did break my stuff, people are always more important than possessions. He was teaching me that while hospitality did invade my personal space, people are always craving a sense of belonging. He was teaching me that while hospitality did eat all my food, people tend to connect best over a shared meal. When God makes room for others within your heart, it's easy for you to make room for them in your home. (From page 117)

A DEEPER LOOK:

- Read Jeremiah 29:4-7.

- Sometimes we may not like where we live or the season of life in which we find ourselves. How does reading Jeremiah's "letter to the exiles" change your perspective on your current situation?

GROUP DISCUSSION:

- Have you ever experimented with biblical hospitality? If so, what was your experience like, and what did God teach you? If not, how can you begin this week?

- Do you find yourself making excuses about why you cannot be hospitable to those around you? Are you willing to share some of those excuses with the group? How can you move past those this week and welcome the stranger?

SMALL GROUP GUIDE: WEEK 6

BEFORE GATHERING:

- Have everyone read *Live S.E.N.T.* chapters 7 and 8.

REFLECTION:

- Which of the "small" gospels have you heard or experienced most often? (Refer to the three "small gospels" in chapter 7 for reference.) What questions, if any, did those variations leave with you? In what ways do you need to adopt a "bigger" gospel?

- In what ways does thinking through the gospel as a story (creation, fall, redemption, restoration) help you understand the Bible's bigger, overall message? How might it help you share the gospel through conversation?

QUOTES:

Just as the story of the Bible starts with creation, every person's life story has a beginning. Just as the story of the Bible speaks about the Fall, every person has experienced brokenness. Just as the story of the Bible anticipates redemption, every person is pursuing betterment in some measure. Just as the story of the Bible longs for restoration, every person hopes for future blessings. (From page 133)

Does this mean the church should never give a gospel presentation? Absolutely not! . . . But it does mean that the church needs to cultivate new habits for talking with people about Jesus. Learning to have ongoing gospel conversations with others models the patient and gracious life that Christ displayed while he lived and walked this earth. By living S.E.N.T., the church can once again talk with others about Jesus in a culturally compelling and Christ-centered way. (From page 142)

A DEEPER LOOK:
- Read Acts 2 and Acts 17:16-34.

- In Acts 2, Peter shares the gospel with a predominantly Jewish audience. In Acts 17, Paul shares the gospel with a predominantly Greek audience. Note the differences and similarities.

- In what ways did they adapt and contextualize the gospel to the surrounding culture? What can we learn from these two passages about how to talk with others about Jesus?

GROUP DISCUSSION:
Challenge: Using the chart on the next page try sharing the gospel as a story (creation, fall, redemption, restoration) with your small group.

The Story of the Gospel	The Story of Our Lives	Answers the Question
Creation	Beginnings	How did I get here?
Fall	Brokenness	Why are things this way?
Redemption	Betterment	What can make life better?
Restoration	Blessings	What will life be like when all is well?

Learning to share and speak with fluency takes practice and time, so be sure to encourage one another along the way. (P.S. If you need help, go back to the four "missional movements" of chapter 1. Those are another useful tool for sharing the gospel as a story.)

APPENDIX C
MORE MEALS OF JESUS

Text	Meal	Guests	Teaching
Matthew 9:9-13	Matthew's Party	Tax collectors and sinners	"I came not to call the righteous, but sinners."
Matthew 12:1-8	Sabbath Snack	Disciples and Pharisees	"For the Son of Man is lord of the Sabbath."
Matthew 14:13-21	Wilderness Feast, Pt. I	Disciples and the multitudes	"They need not go away; you give them something to eat."
Matthew 15:32-39	Wilderness Feast, Pt. II	Disciples and the multitudes	"I have compassion on the crowd because they have been with me now three days and have nothing to eat."
Matthew 26:6-13	Anointed at the Table	Simon the leper, disciples, and an unnamed woman	"Truly, I say to you, wherever this gospel is proclaimed in the whole world, what she has done will also be told in memory of her."
Matthew 26:17-29	Passover/ Last Supper	Disciples	"Take, eat; this is my body. . . Drink of it, all of you, for this is my blood of the covenant, which is poured out for many for the forgiveness of sins."

Text	Meal	Guests	Teaching
Mark 2:13-17	Levi's Party	Tax collectors and sinners	"I came not to call the righteous, but sinners"
Mark 6:30-44	Wilderness Feast, Pt. I	Disciples and the multitudes	"You give them something to eat."
Mark 7:14-23	Messy Meal	Pharisees, scribes, and the disciples	"Hear me, all of you, and understand: There is nothing outside a person that by going into him can defile him, but the things that come out of a person are what defile him."
Mark 8:1-10	Wilderness Feast, Pt. II	Disciples and the multitudes	"I have compassion on the crowd because they have been with me now three days and have nothing to eat."
Mark 14:3-9	Anointed at the Table	Simon the leper, disciples, and an unnamed woman	"And truly, I say to you, wherever the gospel is proclaimed in the whole world, what she has done will be told in memory of her."
Mark 14:12-25	Passover/ Last Supper	Disciples	"Take; this is my body. . . This is my blood of the covenant, which is poured out for many."
Luke 5:27-39	Levi's Party	Tax collectors and sinners	"I have not come to call the righteous but sinners to repentance."

Text	Meal	Guests	Teaching
Luke 7:36-50	Meal at the House of Simon the Pharisee	Pharisees, guests, and a sinful woman	"Your sins are forgiven."
Luke 9:10-17	Wilderness Feast	Disciples and the multitudes	"You give them something to eat."
Luke 10:38-42, NIV	Martha's Meal	Disciples	"Mary has chosen what is better."
Luke 11:37-54	A Dirty Meal	Pharisees and teachers	"You Pharisees cleanse the outside of the cup and of the dish, but inside you are full of greed and wickedness."
Luke 14:1-24	Sabbath Dinner at a Pharisee's house	Pharisees and friends	"When you give a feast, invite the poor, the crippled, the lame, the blind."
Luke 19:1-10	A "Wee Little" Meal	Zacchaeus, tax collectors, and friends	"The Son of Man came to seek and to save the lost."
Luke 22:7-38, NIV	Passover/ Last Supper	Disciples	"And he took bread, gave thanks and broke it, and gave it to them."
Luke 24:13-35, CSB	Meal at Emmaus	Cleopas and another disciple	Jesus was "made known to them in the breaking of the bread."

Text	Meal	Guests	Teaching
Luke 24:36-53	Supper with the Disciples	Disciples	"You are witnesses of these things."
John 2:1-12	Wedding at Cana	Disciples, Jesus's mother, and the wedding guests	Jesus turns water to wine. "But you have kept the good wine until now."
John 4:1-45	A Pit Stop in Samaria	Jesus and a Samaritan woman	"The water that I will give him will become in him a spring of water welling up to eternal life."
John 6:1-15	Wilderness Feast	Disciples and the multitudes	"Where are we to buy bread, so that these people may eat?"
John 12:1-8	Dinner in Bethany	Disciples, Lazarus, Mary, and Martha	"For the poor you always have with you, but you do not always have me."
John 13:1-20	Passover/ Last Supper	Disciples	"If I then, your Lord and Teacher, have washed your feet, you also ought to wash one another's feet."
John 21:15-23	Reinstatement Breakfast	Peter and other disciples	"Follow me."

Acknowledgments

Thank you to those who, long before this book ever came into being, were living S.E.N.T. and challenging my heart to do the same. You saw something long before I did and lived with gospel intentionality within your households, neighborhoods, and cities.

Thank you to my church family, who latched onto living S.E.N.T. from the beginning and allowed it to reorient their lives around the mission of God. I'm forever grateful for a faith community that doesn't merely love in word or talk but in deed and in truth.

Thank you to my immediate family, inspiring friends and those who gave to this project. Each of you are gifts from God.

BIBLIOGRAPHY

Arnold, Jeanne E., Anthony P. Graesch, Enzon Ragazzini, and Elinor Ochs. *Life at Home in the Twenty-First Century: 32 Families Open Their Doors*. Los Angeles, CA: Costen Institute of Archaeology Press. 2017.

Brisco Brad. *ReThink: 9 Paradigm Shifts for Activating the Church*. Alpharetta, GA: SEND Institute, 2015.

Brisco, Brad, and Lance Ford. *Next Door As It Is in Heaven: Living Out God's Kingdom In Your Neighborhood*. Colorado Springs, CO: NavPress, 2016.

Chan, Sam. *Evangelism in a Skeptical World: How to Make the Unbelievable News About Jesus More Believable*. Grand Rapids, MI: Zondervan, 2018.

Chester, Tim. *A Meal with Jesus: Discovering Grace, Community, and Mission Around the Table*. Wheaton, IL: Crossway, 2011.

Cleveland, Christina. *Disunity in Christ: Uncovering the Hidden Forces That Keep Us Apart*. Downers Grove, IL: IVP, 2013.

Darley, John M., and C. Daniel Batson. *From Jerusalem to Jericho: A Study of Situational and Dispositional Variables in Helping Behavior*. Princeton, NJ: Darley, 1970.

Durant, Will. *The Story of Philosophy*. New York: Simon and Schuster, 1961.

Elliot, Jim. *The Journals of Jim Elliot.* Edited by Elizabeth Elliot. Grand Rapids, MI: Revell, 1978.

Finzel, Hans. *The Top Ten Mistakes Leaders Make.* Colorado Springs, CO: David C. Cook, 2007.

Freedman, Russell, and Frédéric Clément. *Confucius: The Golden Rule.* Austin, TX: Holt McDougal. 2006.

Frost, Michael. *Surprise the World!: The Five Habits of Highly Missional People.* Colorado Springs, CO: NavPress, 2016.

Gehring, Roger. *House Church and Mission: The Importance of Household Structures in Early Christianity.* Peabody, MA: Hendrickson, 2004.

Gensler, Harry. *Ethics and the Golden Rule: Do Unto Others.* New York: Routledge, 2013.

Halter, Hugh. *Flesh: Bringing the Incarnation Down to Earth.* Colorado Springs, CO: David C. Cook, 2014.

Halter, Hugh, and Matt Smay. *AND: The Gathered and Scattered Church.* Grand Rapids, MI: Zondervan, 2013.

Halter, Hugh, and Matt Smay. *The Tangible Kingdom: Creating Incarnational Community.* San Francisco, CA: Jossey-Bass, 2008.

Hardy, Darren. *The Compound Effect: Jumpstart Your Income, Your Life, Your Success.* Boston, MA: Da Capo Press. 2010.

Hilton, Allen. "Living into the Big Story: The Missional Trajectory of Scripture in Congregational Life." In *Cultivating Sent* Communities, edited by Dwight J. Zscheile. Grand Rapids, MI: Eerdman's, 2012.

Hirsch, Alan, and Lance Ford. *Right Here, Right Now: Everyday Mission for Everyday People.* Grand Rapids, MI: Baker Books, 2011.

Missional Church Consultation and Dwight J. Zscheile. *Cultivating Sent Communities: Missional Spiritual Formation.* Grand Rapids, MI: Eerdmans, 2012.

Putnam, Robert. *Bowling Alone: The Collapse and Revival of American Community.* New York: Simon and Schuster, 2000.

Rogers, Fred. 1994. Quoted in Tyler Huckabee, "11 Mr. Rogers Quotes Every Christian Should Read." *Relevant Magazine,* 2019.

Runyon, Dave, and Jay Pathak. *The Art of Neighboring: Building Genuine Relationships Right Outside Your Door.* Grand Rapids, MI: Baker Books, 2012.

Swindoll, Chuck. *Insights on John: Swindoll's New Testament Insights.* Grand Rapids, MI: Zondervan. 2010.

Vanderstelt, Jeff. *Saturate: Being Disciples of Jesus in the Everyday Stuff of Life.* Wheaton, IL: Crossway, 2015.

Willis, Dustin, and Brandon Clements. *The Simplest Way to Change the World: Biblical Hospitality as a Way of Life.* Chicago: Moody, 2017.

Wright, Christopher J.H. *The Mission of God's People: A Biblical Theology of the Church's Mission.* Grand Rapids, MI: Zondervan. 2010.